Confident that God can use
this book to bless your life
it has been given to you
by the author

Searching Questions

Searching Questions

Robert E. McNeill B.A., B.D., D.D.

WINEPRESS WP PUBLISHING

Packaged by WinePress Publishing, PO Box 428, Enumclaw, WA 98022. The views expressed or implied in this work do not necessarily reflect those of WinePress Publishing. The author(s) is ultimately responsible for the design, content and editorial accuracy of this work.

Unless otherwise stated, all scripture references are taken from the King James Version of the Bible.

ISBN 1-57921-751-6
Library of Congress Catalog Card Number: 2004093201

This book is gratefully dedicated to my

CHILDREN'S CHILDREN

Neil Hitchcock, Betsy Foster, Heather Kinnamon, Haddon McKinney, Heidi McKinney, Hope McKinney, Suzanne McNeill, Stephanie McNeill, Sophie McNeill, Jolinda McNeill, Madison McNeill.

But the mercy of the Lord is from
everlasting to everlasting
Upon them that fear him
And his righteousness unto
children's children.

Psalm 103:17

What a promise! Mercy and righteousness are two of the greatest words in the Bible and these two great blessings will be bestowed upon grandchildren if parents and their children fear God. No wonder that Solomon, David's son, wrote these words:

Children's children are the crown of old men:
And the glory of children are their fathers.

Proverbs 17:6

The Doctrines of Sovereign Grace
by Charles Haddon Spurgeon

You cannot vanquish a Calvinist. You may think you can, but you cannot. The stones of the great doctrines so fit into each other, that the more pressure there is applied to remove them the more strenuously do they adhere. And you may mark, that you cannot receive one of these doctrines without believing all.

Hold for instance that man is utterly depraved, and you draw the inference then that certainly if God has such a creature to deal with salvation must come from God alone, and if from him, the offended one, to an offending creature, then he has a right to give or withhold his mercy as he wills; you are thus forced upon election, and when you have gotten that you have all: the others must follow.

Some by putting the strain upon their judgments may manage to hold two or three points and not the rest, but sound logic I take it requires a man to hold the whole or reject the whole; the doctrines stand like soldiers in a square, presenting on every side a line of defense which is hazardous to attack, but easy to maintain.

And mark you, in these times when error is so rife and theology strives to be so rampant, it is no little thing to put into the hands of a young man a weapon which can slay his foe, which he can easily learn to handle, which he may grasp tenaciously, wield readily, and carry without fatigue; a weapon, I may add, which no rust can corrode and no blows can break, trenchant, and well annealed, a true Jerusalem blade of a temper fit for deeds of renown. [1]

---

[1] C.H. Spurgeon, "Exposition of the Doctrines of Grace," in The Metropolitan Tabernacle Pulpit (Pasadena, Texas: Pilgrim Publications, 1969) Vol 7, p. 304

TABLE OF CONTENTS

Introduction: The Value of Questions 11

Chapter 1:   Why So Significant? 15
Chapter 2:   Who Was the Ultimate Prophet? 29
Chapter 3:   Why Did Paul the Apostle Suffer So Much? 43
Chapter 4:   Does the Bible Teach a Free Offer of the Gospel? 61
Chapter 5:   What Is Salvation? 73
Chapter 6:   Who Was Responsible for Christ's Death? 85
Chapter 7:   Is It Free Will or Free Grace? 99
Chapter 8:   Does Prophecy Have Pivotal Passages? 111
Chapter 9:   What Was Christ's Greatest Declaration? 129
Chapter 10: Are You Happy? 145
Chapter 11: What Is Life's Greatest Truth? 161
Chapter 12: Is a Resurrection Incredible? 175
Chapter 13: What Is the Fruit of Justification? 189

"How do you know so much about everything?" was asked of a very wise and intelligent man; and his answer was, "By never being afraid or ashamed to ask questions as to anything of which I was ignorant."

Jacob Abbott

THE VALUE OF QUESTIONS

by George M. Bowman

All scripture is given by inspiration of God, and is profitable for doctrine, for reproof, for correction, for instruction in righteousness: That the man of God may be perfect, throughly furnished unto all good works.

(2 Timothy 3:16–17)

It seems to be a common experience among Christians to have questions about the Bible they find difficult to answer. Since launching Operation Balance—a personal, nonprofit, writing and publishing ministry to advance sound doctrine that holds biblical truth in balance—I have received many letters from pastors, educators, and lay Christians with questions about these topics: Bible versions, creation vs. evolution, the new birth, the local church, various doctrines, modern methods of evangelism, the role of the Holy Spirit, prayer, prophecy, Satan, worship, and biblical interpretation.

Rightly Interpreted, the Bible Has the Answers

I found that most of the problems my correspondents had with biblical questions came from reading and studying the Bible through filters of personal prejudices or erroneous systems of doctrine. I also saw that such read-through filters can often raise more questions than answers.

In my own experience, I found that learning how to interpret the Bible made it much easier to find its answers to difficult questions. Though the Bible does say it contains "some things hard to be understood" (2 Peter 3:16), it also contains much that is easily learned and can be applied in a practical way to the Christian life. "All scripture," said Paul, "is given by inspiration of God, and is profitable for doctrine, for reproof, for correction, for instruction in righteousness: That the man of God may be perfect, throughly furnished unto all good works" (2 Timothy 3:16–17).

Increasing Curiosity

I once heard a preacher say, "The best way to get a good education is to be a question mark seeking the answers to thoughtful questions."

Ever since my conversion to Christ more than 57 years ago, I have had an increasing curiosity to know the Bible's answers to many questions. Seeking those answers is what motivated me to build a substantial library and become a Christian writer so I could share the answers I found with others.

On every subject, I wanted to know not necessarily what the most popular religious leaders and writers had to say, but what the Bible *actually* said. Having read a great many books, including *The Westminster Shorter Catechism*, I know that it is spiritually profitable to read a book that asks and answers searching questions about the Bible.

Walking on Holy Ground

As I worked as editor of Dr. McNeill's book, *Searching Questions*, I felt that I was walking on holy ground. May the Lord give you a similar reaction to its contents. Dr. McNeill writes from the conviction that the Bible is the infallible and authoritative Word of almighty God. He is also a champion of the sound doctrines of sovereign grace, and it is with those doctrines in mind as a biblical backdrop that he writes.

As a veteran preacher of the gospel, and a pastor called to edify the saints, his sincere desire and prayer is that this book will move you to take an increasing interest in the Word of God as the most interesting and challenging and profitable book in print.

The topics of this book are provocative in the sense that, using the effective educational device of questions and answers, they will provoke you to think seriously about them. Dr. McNeill does not pretend to provide answers to all the questions one might ask about the contents of the Bible. If you are a Christian with a mature curiosity that looks constantly for answers to questions about biblical topics, however, you will enjoy your study of the searching questions and answers given in this book.

May God's blessed Holy Spirit use what you read here to increase your knowledge of his infallible and eternal Word, and encourage you to think more deeply about the level of your relationship and commitment to his Son, the Lord Jesus Christ. I am convinced that your reading of this book will increase your knowledge of the Bible. I am also convinced that the more one knows about the triune God and his Word, the more he will strive to live in loving obedience to the precepts of Jesus Christ and give himself over to promoting his glorious cause.

CHAPTER ONE

WHY SO SIGNIFICANT?

For who maketh thee to differ from another? and what hast thou that thou didst not receive? Now if thou didst receive it, why dost thou glory, as if thou hadst not received it?

(1 Corinthians 4:7)

The Bible asks hundreds of questions. Some of these are of the utmost importance not only for our physical life, but for what we believe about the gift of eternal life and the heavenly prospects of the Christian life. Job 38 has 35 questions—more than any other chapter of the Bible.

Some of these questions have staggered the greatest scientific minds of our day. For example, ponder these creation questions: "Have you entered into the springs of the sea? Have you walked in the search of the depth? Where is the way where light dwelleth? Have you entered into the treasures of the snow?"

The First and Last Questions

The first question in the Bible was part of the tempting words by Satan that prompted Eve to sin and brought God's judgment curse upon the whole creation. He asked, "Yea, hath God said, Ye shall not eat of every tree of the garden?"

Though the first question in the Old Testament is asked by Satan, the last question of the Old Testament is one that God says men were asking about him: "You have said, It is vain to serve God: and what profit is it that we have kept his ordinance, and that we have walked mournfully before the Lord of hosts?" (Malachi 3:14).

The first question of the New Testament is a question concerning the Lord Jesus Christ. In Matthew 2:2, the wise men from the east ask, "Where is he that is born King of the Jews?" And an angel asks the last question of the Word of God. The Lord had shown John the apostle the vision of the harlot city that was guilty of murdering many saints. Seeing it, he wonders with great admiration. "Wherefore," asks the angel, "didst thou marvel?" (Revelation 17:7).

Questions about Salvation

Many theologians would say that the most important questions of the Bible would deal with a sinner's salvation, such as these:

- What shall I do then with Jesus which is called Christ?
- What think ye of Christ?
- What shall it profit a man if he should gain the whole world and lose his own soul?
- What shall a man give in exchange for his soul?
- What must I do to be saved?

The book of Job, which some Bible authorities believe is one of the oldest books in the Bible, has similar questions:

- If a man die shall he live again?
- How then can man be justified with God? or how can he be clean that is born of a woman?

Three Questions by Paul

As important and soul-searching as some of these questions are, there is a group of three questions found in 1 Corinthians 4:7 that are as thought-provoking as any in all the Bible. They are all-important because they make the reader center his or her thoughts on God Almighty.

Some questions can be answered without too much thought. But these questions, inspired by the Holy Spirit of God and written by Paul the apostle, should make every Christian humble, thankful, and full of praise. These questions should make even an unbeliever think. Here are those three questions:

- Who maketh thee to differ from another?
- What hast thou that thou didst not receive?
- Why dost thou glory, as if thou hadst not received it?

Newspaper journalists use what they call the five-W formula for writing news stories. Those five Ws stand for Who, What, When, Where, and Why. Every lead of a well-written news story will answer those five questions:

1. Who is involved?
2. What happened?
3. When did it happen?
4. Where did it happen?
5. Why did it happen?

In Paul the apostle's three questions to the Corinthian Christians, he used three of those five Ws: Who, What, and Why. "Who maketh thee to differ from another?" "What hast thou that thou didst not receive?" "Why dost thou glory, as if thou hadst not received it?"

WHO MAKETH THEE TO DIFFER FROM ANOTHER?

The Absurdity of Pride

In the original Greek, this question could read, "For who distinguishes you?" or "Who gives you distinguishing and discriminating grace and mercy?" In this question, Paul was aiming at the sin of pride, which is one of the most common sins committed by man.

Pride is not only the most foolish of all sins, it is a very destructive sin. For example, a man is not proud because he is rich; he is proud because he is richer than someone else. A beautiful woman is not proud because she is beautiful; she is proud because she is more beautiful than someone else. A successful businessman is not proud because he is successful; he is proud because he is more successful than some other businessman. The whole aim of pride is to put others down, which in essence is a desire to destroy them.

A hundred arguments might be used to show the absurdity of pride, but none would be sufficient to quench its vitality. Human nature, or "the flesh" as the Bible calls it, will always entertain pride to some degree. Even those who profess faith in Christ are often guilty of the sin of pride, because most of us Christians do such a poor job of mortifying the flesh and getting rid of pride.

Creation itself speaks against our pride. Paul used the example of the potter and the clay to show the utter foolishness of replying to God the Creator. Does the clay say to the potter, "Why hast thou made me thus?" Of course not. Yet human beings, who were fashioned by God the Creator, have a tendency to ask him why he created them as they are. Men are nothing but dust or clay in the hands of God, and because he is the creator God, he has the right to fashion them as he desired.

The Bible shows the great contrast between God and his creatures when it says, "God that sitteth upon the circle of the earth, and the inhabitants thereof are as grasshoppers; that stretcheth out the heavens as a curtain, and spreadeth them out as a tent to dwell in" (Isaiah 40:22).

The Sin of Self-Importance

Do you ever suffer from a feeling of self-importance? Believe the words of Isaiah 40:15–18, and you will change your mind about self-importance. In those verses the prophet wrote,

> Behold, the nations are as a drop of a bucket, and are counted as the small dust of the balance: behold, he taketh up the isles as a very little thing. And Lebanon is not sufficient to burn, nor the beasts thereof sufficient for a burnt offering. All nations before him are as nothing; and they are counted by him less than nothing, and vanity. To whom then will ye liken God? or what likeness will you compare unto him?

In the light of such profound and pregnant words, how can we logically believe that we have the right to be proud and self-important? If all the nations of the world are as a drop in a bucket, as the dust on the scales, as nothing, or as less than nothing and vanity, how can we as the individuals, who make up the nations, think that we are important in God's sight?

Anne Graham Lotz, daughter of Billy Graham, made a grave error about herself when she said that Christ "the most important man in the universe thinks I am so important, he gave his life for me! ... In the eyes of the Lord Jesus Christ I am important. I am of value. How can I consider myself anything less?" (*The Vision of His Glory*, p. 13). Here is a comment on these words of Mrs. Lotz:

> Christ did not give his life for elect sinners because he thought they were important, but because they had been predestinated and given to him by God on the proviso that he would die in their place to redeem them. And he gave himself for them, not because they were important, but because he loved them and wanted to rescue them from their helpless and hopeless estate.

Once we get the idea that we are important, we deny what the Bible says about us. The only thing of value in us as Christians is what God has given to us in Jesus Christ. Humility before God is a more biblical attitude than a feeling of importance.[1]

Like a Dagger

What audacity there is in human sinners to think they have the right to question God, to complain about their circumstances, or to murmur against the God of all creation! "Who maketh thee to differ from another?" This question should be like a dagger put to the throat of our attitudes of pride and self-importance. Each of us should ask himself this question: "If I am saved, if I am a Christian, if I have been given light, if my sinful heart has been opened, search now the question, who made me to differ from others who are now still wallowing in their sin?"

God's Providential Dealings

Many of us differ from others in God's providential dealings. I have a thanksgiving prayer that I've been praying well over a half a century, a prayer I prayed as a child and as an unbeliever. "God, I thank you that I was born in the United States of America."

When we think of the poverty, the ignorance, the superstition, and the oppression in many countries of the world, what a privilege, what a blessing to have been born in an enlightened country! Think of the grace of God that has made us to differ even from many of our own countrymen.

According to the U.S. Census report of 2001, about 33 million or 11.7 percent of Americans live in poverty. Are we thankful for God's providential dealings in national, parental, and circumstantial events in our lives? What about the sick and the suffering in hospitals? Some have lain on sick beds for 5, 10, or 15 years. Having been delivered from many calamities that others suffer, do we

---

[1]George M. Bowman, *Blurred Visions* (Whitby, Ontario: Operation Balance, 2002), 44.

give our blessings little thought, or are we daily thankful to God for making us to differ?

God's Inexhaustible Grace

Have you ever sat in a church service and remembered what it was like a few years ago? Like many church attenders you were careless, hardened, and thoughtless about your own salvation. The sacred music and the gospel sermon fell on ears that were not listening. Why do your ears and heart now welcome gospel words and the great hymns of the church? Who made you to differ? Did you make yourself to differ? No, it is like the poet said,

> *Twas the same love which spread the feast*
> *That sweetly forced us in:*
> *Else we had still refused to taste,*
> *And perished in our sin.*

All believers should be crying out with those of old, "His work is honourable and glorious: and His righteousness endureth for ever" (Psalm 111:3).

Former Associates

As a Christian, do you ever think about some of your cronies, companions, teammates, friends of former years who are yet unsaved and show no interest in the things of the Lord? Do you ask yourself, "What made me to differ?" More than once I've thought of an incident in my college days when I received a much-deserved rebuke from a college fraternity brother and fellow football teammate. He was the best football player I ever played with or against, a little All-American. He was a number of years older than I, and had come to college much later than right out of high school, and was working hard to earn his college degree.

His parents were dead, whereas my parents came down to college and even to our out-of-town games to see me play. Both of us were unsaved. One morning we were alone at the breakfast table.

He quietly, but firmly rebuked me for my swearing, gambling, and deportment. He also criticized me for my lack of appreciation for the college education my parents were giving me.

I never forgot his stern rebuke. Three years later, God used a football injury to lead me to repentance and faith in Jesus Christ. The sad part of the whole story was he never learned of my salvation. He died in World War II when the ship on which he was serving went down in the Pacific. "Who made thee," I asked myself, "to differ from another?"

Backsliders

Do we ever think seriously about God's part in our redemption and the testimony of his grace in our lives? Why do some Christians ruin their profession of faith in Christ by participating in some scandalous sin, and why are some kept from doing so? What causes them to differ?

Some Christians make the mistake of believing in sinless perfection or the possibility of total eradication of the sinful nature in Christians. For example, Gary L. Cutler, author of *Facing End-Time Reality*, has these words about himself on page 2 of his book: "He was converted on the Birmingham Free Methodist campground at the age of eight, later **entirely sanctified**, and called into the Christian ministry while still a teenager" (emphasis added).

According to the Bible, no one is "entirely sanctified" in this life because sanctification is the progressive realization of complete holiness—a goal no Christian can reach until he gets to heaven. Those who believe and preach sinless perfection or entire sanctification or the eradication of sin in this life must have some difficulty with the sins of godly men like Noah, Lot, David, Solomon, and Peter. The hymn writer was much wiser when he wrote,

Ah, Lord: with such a heart as mine,
Unless you hold me fast,
I feel I must, I shall decline
And prove like them at last.

Who maketh thee to differ? If God alone has made you to differ, why may he not make others to differ too? After he was saved, one notorious sinner said, "After the Lord saved me, I never despaired of anybody."

WHAT HAST THOU THAT THOU DIDST NOT RECEIVE?

Unthankful Recipients

Isn't it amazing how many men and women there are who get puffed up over some natural talent or gift they received? For example how many athletes are there who thank God for their speed and physique? Muhammad Ali, the former heavy weight boxing champion of the world was so self-centered that he used to boast, "I am the greatest." Think of the many famous opera singers who are so proud of their voices, they never think of praising God for their wonderful gifts.

"A man can receive nothing," said John the Baptist, "except it be given him from heaven" (John 3:27). How helpful in spiritual growth it would be for every student to memorize that verse? What John said also applies to the salvation of sinners, in which they receive eternal life. "For the wages of sin is death," said Paul, "but the gift of God is eternal life through Jesus Christ our Lord" (Romans 6:23).

Though unbelievers never thank God for what they have received from him, that should not be the case with us who have received eternal life from him. Knowing what we know, we should daily thank the Lord for everything we have, because he is the giver of all.

"Every good gift and every perfect gift," said James, "is from above, and cometh down from the Father of lights, with whom is no variableness, neither shadow of turning. Of his own will begat he us with the word of truth, that we should be a kind of first fruits of his creatures" (James 1:17–18).

The Testimony of Augustine

Augustine was one of the greatest theologians of the early church. The Lord used 1 Corinthians 4:7, the passage we are discussing in this chapter, to change Augustine from his belief in synergism—that salvation was a co-operative effort between God and man—to a belief in monergism which literally means "one work." Some have the idea that they were born again because they repented and believed in Christ. In other words, they believe that their repentance and faith were the cause of their new birth. Not so. Repentance and faith, and conviction of sin and guilt are gifts from God that are the results, not the cause, of the new birth. The regeneration of a sinner is the sovereign and exclusive work of the Holy Spirit. Here is Augustine's testimony on the subject:

It was especially by this passage [1 Corinthians 4:7] that I myself also was convinced when I erred in a similar manner thinking that the faith by which we believe in God is not the gift of God, but that it is in us of ourselves, and that by it we obtain the gifts of God whereby we may live temperately, and righteously and piously in this world. Nor I did not think that faith was preceded by God's grace, but to consent after the Gospel had been preached to us, I thought belonged to ourselves, and came to us from ourselves.

How can it be explained that the Gospel reaches one man and not another? and that even the same dispensations act quite differently on different persons? It belongs to God to furnish the means which led every man to believe, consequently the reason of the difference can only be that according to his own decree, it seems good to withhold it from one and not from another. All men in consequence of the first transgression are exposed to perdition; in this state there can be no higher movement therefore, none at all in them towards conversion.

WHY DOST THOU GLORY AS IF THOU HADST NOT RECEIVED IT?

The Sovereignty of God

This third question that Paul asked was more than adequately covered by the prophet who gave God-given advice in Jeremiah 9:23–24:

> Thus saith the LORD, Let not the wise man glory in his wisdom, neither let the mighty man glory in his might, let not the rich man glory in his riches, But let him who glories glory in this, that he understandeth and knoweth me, that I am the Lord which exercises loving kindness, judgment, and righteousness in the earth: for in these things I delight, saith the LORD.

This passage of God's Word says that the sovereignty of God should humble us to the effect that we do not allow ourselves to be puffed up or to glory in ourselves or in anything we do or accomplish. No doctrine exalts or magnifies God and the finished work of Christ's redemption as that of God's sovereignty. Therefore it should be reasonable for us to believe that God, "worketh all things after the counsel of his own will" (Ephesians 1:11).

Revealed in the Bible

The Bible says we are "not to think of men above that which is written, that no one of you be puffed up, one against another" (1 Corinthians 4:6). The one major reason for believing in the absolute, universal sovereignty of God is the fact that it is revealed in the Bible. It is the only book in the world that originally revealed this unqualified truth. Why this is so is very simple.

The Bible is distinctly and exclusively the Word and Work of God: all other books are more or less the words and works of men. The cause of one's faith in the unmodified "sovereignty of

God" as revealed in the Bible is that it is *divinely given* unto him to believe it. That is, the gracious sovereignty of God makes a person believe it.

The reality of this truth is most distinctly and most certainly set forth throughout the Bible. Though they do not intend it to be so, the fact that men, religious or irreligious, oppose and seek to distort God's sovereignty to suit their feelings and fancies, is one of the best testimonies to its truth.

God in his glorious sovereignty, whom men rail against, has not yet condescended to give them that grace which is needed to humble them and make them willing and able to heartily believe that which he has written. "So then, it is not of him that willeth," wrote Paul, "nor of him that runneth, but of God who shews mercy" (Romans 9:16).

Testimony of a Theologian

John L. Dagg, writer, pastor and college president (Mercer University) says that God's sovereign acts are not pursued without reference to a wise and good pleasure. God's pleasure is always good, because it is directed to the end of manifesting his own nature. Dagg says God

> is sovereign in his acts, because his acts are determined by his own perfections. He has a rule for what he does; but this rule is not prescribed to him by any other being, nor does it exist independently of himself. It is found in his own nature. In his acts, his nature is unfolded and displayed. (*Manual of Theology*, p. 305)

Known, But Not Comprehended

Can we find words to magnify the name of our great God as he ought to be magnified? In prayer, David saw a vast difference between God the Creator of all things and man. "When I consider thy heavens, the work of thy fingers, the moon and the stars, which thou hast ordained; what is man that thou art mindful of him?"

(Psalm 8:3–4). In the light of God's creation, he saw man as minute by comparison.

Isaiah showed how impossible it is to comprehend God. "The Creator of the ends of the earth," he said, "fainteth not, neither is weary, there is no searching his understanding" (Isaiah 40:28).

We may know God, but it is impossible for us to comprehend him. Our knowledge of God is like the point of a pin on a globe of the earth. The pin knows the globe, but it cannot comprehend it. We are allowed to know as much about God as he has revealed of himself in his Word, but because we are finite and God is infinite, we can never comprehend him.

Nothing Exalts God as Does His Sovereignty

Solomon, the wisest man who ever lived, had a bigger than average knowledge of God. "Whatsoever God doeth," he said, "it shall be for ever: nothing can be put to it, nor anything taken from it: and God doeth it, that men should fear before him" (Ecclesiastes 3:14). The very works of God should cause all men to realize how great he is and to bow before him in reverential fear.

Is there any other doctrine or anything else, that so exalts God as does his sovereignty, his right to do as he pleases with his own? God told Moses in Exodus 19:5 that all the earth was his. God told Ezekiel, "All souls are mine; as the soul of the father, so also the soul of the son is mine: the soul that sinneth, it shall die" (Ezekiel 18:4).

You and I are accountable to a great God! That is why hundreds of years after Ezekiel, the Lord Jesus asked two important questions: "For what shall it profit a man, if he shall gain the whole world, and lose his soul? Or what shall a man give in exchange for his soul?" (Mark 8:36–37).

Nothing magnifies his love in the heart of a saved sinner as his sovereignty. The wicked appreciate not God's love for they know nothing of it. It is only those who have been made the objects of his divine choice and spiritual regeneration who can know the real love of God and praise him for it. God's sovereignty is indispensable to his existence as the God of creation, providence and redemption. God's sovereignty magnifies his redemptive love for his own people as nothing else can do.

The next time someone asks you how you were saved, do not neglect to show God's sovereignty in your salvation. Don't make the mistake of exalting yourself as most testimonies do. Over and over we hear personal testimonies that say something like this: "Letting Jesus Christ into my heart was the smartest decision I ever made." Instead say, "I was saved by God's grace alone through his gift of faith alone in Jesus Christ alone."

To show that faith is a gift from God, you might quote Ephesians 2:8–9: "For by grace are ye saved through faith; and that [faith] not of yourselves: it [the faith] is the gift of God: not of works, lest any man should boast." Salvation, then is not *by* faith, but *through* faith.

It is God who saves. And the means he used was the righteous life, vicarious death or shed blood, and triumphant resurrection of his Son, Jesus Christ. Christ ascended to heaven after his resurrection to rule over all creation and to make intercession for his people.

Alexander MacLaren put it this way: "Faith is simply the channel through which there flows over into my emptiness the divine fullness. It is not faith that saves us; it is Christ that saves us and saves us *through* Faith."

If you have received that gift of faith from God and are rejoicing in your new position with Christ, ask yourself this question, "Who made me to differ from somebody else?" Then thank the Lord for making you a citizen of his kingdom and a member of his royal family.

CHAPTER TWO

WHO WAS THE ULTIMATE PROPHET?

The Lord thy God will raise up unto thee a Prophet from the midst
of you, of thy brethren, like unto me; unto him ye shall hearken.
(Deuteronomy 18:15)

Approximately 1,450 years before the Lord Jesus Christ was born in Bethlehem of Judea, a prophecy about him was made by Moses, one of the greatest men who ever walked on the face of the earth. He was on the plains of Moab, east of the Jordan River, speaking to the people of Israel. It was just prior to his death and burial by the Lord on Mount Nebo. "The Lord thy God," he said, "will raise up unto thee a Prophet from the midst of thee, of your brethren, like unto me; unto him ye shall hearken" (Deuteronomy 18:15).

They Never Forgot

The children of Israel apostatized and disobeyed the laws and statutes of God, which he had given through Moses. Because of their unbelief and idolatry, God punished them over and over again. Many of them were killed in battle with other nations.

Thousands were carried into captivity. The nation of Israel was harassed by Philistines, Ammonites, Egyptians, Syrians, Medo-Persians, Assyrians, Greeks, and Romans. But over many generations, the nation of Israel never forgot Moses' words before his death. They believed that some time in their future God would raise up another great prophet like unto Moses.

John the Baptist Interrogated

Fourteen to fifteen centuries is a long time to remember an utterance by a by-gone leader, but this statement by Moses the law giver is alluded to no less than six times in the New Testament. John 1:19–21 says that priests and Levites came to enquire of John the Baptist. "Who art thou?" they asked.

> And he confessed, and denied not; but confessed, "I am not the Christ."
> And they asked him, "What then? Art thou Elijah?"
> And he saith, "I am not."
> "Art thou that prophet?"
> And he answered, "No."

Two Things Worth Noticing

As we read this dialogue between Jewish leaders and John the Baptist, we cannot help but see that two specific things are worth noticing. First, after centuries of history, unbelieving priests and Levites were looking for that prophet. They had heard John the Baptist saying, "Repent ye: for the kingdom of heaven is at hand" (Matthew 3:2). So they asked him point blank, "Art thou that prophet?"

Their question is understandable. John the Baptist was a godly man of great oratorical power, and men could not help but be impressed by his appearance and preaching. The Lord Jesus himself said, "Among them that are born of women there hath not risen a greater than John the Baptist" (Matthew 11:11).

The second thing to notice is that those religious unbelievers did not identify the Messiah with that prophet. In John 1:20, John

30

the Baptist had said definitely that he was not the Christ or Messiah. Yet they asked him, "Art thou that Prophet?" Evidently they thought that Christ and "that prophet" were two different persons.

Similar to Today's Liberals

Is this not the same mistake made by modernists and liberals of our day? They want to admit that Jesus of Nazareth was a great man, a prophet no doubt, but certainly not the Messiah from heaven who was both God and man. "He was a good man," they say, "but he was not God."

They refuse to believe in his virgin birth, his supernatural powers, his vicarious life, his sacrificial death, and his triumphant resurrection. Neither do they believe that Christ ascended to heaven as the sovereign ruler and judge of all creation. It is no wonder that their churches are filled with people making a false profession of a counterfeit faith. A church's congregation will rise no higher spiritually than that of the minister.

Three More References

One of Christ's own apostles identified Christ with the prophet whose coming was foretold by Moses and the other prophets. Philip was so excited about meeting Christ that he went looking for Nathanael. When he found him, he said, "We have found him, of whom Moses in the law, and the prophets, did write, Jesus of Nazareth, the son of Joseph" (John 1:45).

The next identification of Christ with "that prophet" was made by some of the 5,000 Jews in Galilee whom Jesus had just supernaturally fed with only five loaves and two fish. When they saw Jesus perform that amazing miracle, they said, "This is of a truth that prophet that should come into the world" (John 6:14).

The fourth reference to Christ as "that prophet" was at the Feast of Tabernacles in Jerusalem. Christ had just preached, "If any man thirst, let him come unto me, and drink. He that believeth on me, as the scripture hath said, out of his belly shall flow rivers of living water" (John 7:37–38).

31

By the grace of God many were so moved by what Jesus had said, that they said, "Of a truth this is the Prophet" (John 7:40). They were obviously impressed when they heard this tremendous offer by Christ. But they merely said, "This is the Prophet." The Bible does not say that they received him as such. Words are cheap and worth little unless followed by action.

How true this is of our day! Many make decisions for Christ and claim to be born again Christians whose lives do not manifest their possession of a new spiritual life from God the Holy Spirit. They make the grave mistake of thinking that a momentary profession of faith means the possession of eternal life! They do not realize that one cannot be justified if he is not also sanctified. The Bible says they must pursue holiness because "without holiness no man shall see the Lord" (Hebrews 12:14).

Sermons by Peter and Stephen

Let's review quickly. After 1500 years, unbelieving priests and Levities, one of Christ's own apostles, Galileans and Jews from Jerusalem in the temple are all saying that Jesus of Nazareth is "that Prophet" whom Moses predicted would come. But the Lord used two men and their sermons which are recorded in Acts to positively declare that the Lord Jesus Christ was the fulfillment of Moses' prediction.

After healing the lame man at the gate of the temple in the name of Jesus, Peter accused his Jewish listeners of murdering the Lord Jesus, the Prince of life. He also said, "Repent ye therefore, and be converted, that your sins may be blotted out" (Acts 3:19).

Then he said, "For Moses truly said unto the fathers, A prophet shall the Lord, your God, raise up unto you of your brethren, like unto me; him shall ye hear in all things, whatsoever he shall say unto you" (Acts 3:22). In effect, he was saying that Jesus Christ whom they had murdered was alive, and he was the prophet that Moses said would come.

The second sermon was by Stephen who preached it before the Jewish leaders. After preaching Jesus Christ to them, he said that Jesus was the prophet whose appearance was predicted by Moses (Acts 7:37).

He also said, "Which of the prophets have not your fathers persecuted? and they have slain them which shewed before of the coming of the Just One; of whom ye have been now the betrayers and murderers."

When Stephen said that the Just One was that Prophet, and they had killed him, it was too much for the Jews. They ground their teeth in anger at him, refused to listen to Stephen, and all together they ran upon him. They dragged him out of the city and formed a ring around him to stone him to death. As the stones smashed against his arms and legs and torso and head, he knelt down and cried with a loud voice, "Lord, lay not this sin to their charge." Then he fell over dead. The Jews were so wicked that they murdered a godly man for telling the truth![2]

Prophet, Priest, and King

The Lord Jesus Christ, the greatest of all the prophets, was persecuted and murdered like the rest of the prophets. His death, however, was different because he died that sinners like us may have eternal life.

The mediatorial work of Christ is often referred to as the three offices of "Prophet, Priest, and King." In him those offices are indivisible. They cannot be divided as they were among the prophets, priests, and kings in the days of the Old Testament. Apart from one exception, those three offices were never found united in one man other than Jesus. Melchizedek was a king and priest, but not a prophet; Aaron was prophet and priest, but not a king; David and Solomon were kings and prophets, but not priests.

The only man before Christ who was prophet, priest, and king was Moses. He seems to be the one exception yet we are not sure that all these offices were his at the same time in his life. He certainly was a prophet, for none like him arose until the Messiah came. He was a king in Jeshurun (Deuteronomy 33:5), and he officiated as a priest before his brother Aaron was invested with the office. After that, however, Moses never functioned as a priest.

---

[2]For more on this godly man, see the book, *STEPHEN: A Biblical Example of What it Means to Live and Die for Jesus Christ*, by George M. Bowman.

In Christ all three offices meet in a wonderful way. He is a Prophet mighty in deed and word, he is a Priest after the order of Melchizedek, and he is King of Kings and Lord of Lords.

Theologian A.A. Hodge said, "The offices of Christ as prophet, priest and king are like the several functions of one living human body. Lungs, heart, brain are functionally distinct, yet interdependent, and together constituting one life. The functions of prophet, priest and king mutually imply one another: Christ is always a prophetical Priest, and a priestly Prophet; and he is always a royal Priest and a priestly King; and together they accomplish one redemption, to which all are equally essential." Another commentator says,

> The names given to our Saviour in Hebrews 13 by the author are Lord, Jesus, Christ, and that great shepherd of the sheep. These names point to his three offices of King, Priest, and Prophet. We cannot glorify him and manifest his pre-eminence in our lives unless we are determined to acknowledge him in all of his offices. And that means we must practice self-denial and see in him our all in all.

> He is the God of creation; we are his creatures. He is the everlasting King; we are his subjects. He is the Saviour; we are the saved. He is our great High Priest; we are the reconciled. He is the Prophet; we are the recipients of his truth. He is the Messiah; we are the new Israel for whom he was cut off (Daniel 9:26). He is the Good Shepherd; we are the sheep of his pasture. There is no room for self exaltation in a recognition of our Lord Jesus Christ as he is represented in all of these titles.

> Today this kind of recognition is severely lacking among professing Christians. We need to get back to the biblical way of professing identity with our glorious Saviour as Prophet, Priest and King. What great changes there would be in our churches

if all believers surrendered themselves to Jesus Christ in all of
his offices![3]

SCRIPTURAL DEFINITION
OF A PROPHET

The Meaning of the Word

Today when the word "prophet" is used in America, the vast
majority of people immediately associate the idea of predicting
future events. In the biblical sense of the word, we must avoid this
narrow interpretation, which would make the prophet a mere fore-
teller of future events. The true scriptural prophet was rather an
inspired interpreter or revealer of the divine will, a medium of
communication between God and man.

In the Old Testament, there are three different Hebrew words
for our English word "prophet." In Exodus 7:1 and Deuteronomy
18:18, we see that one of these Hebrew words designates "one who
comes with a message from God to the people." The other two
Hebrew words stress the fact that the prophet is "one who receives
revelations from God, particularly in the form of visions."

These words are used interchangeably. Other designations for
a prophet were "man of God," "Messenger of the Lord," and "watch-
man." All these appellatives indicate that the prophets were in the
special service of the Lord, and watched for the spiritual interests
of the people.

In the New Testament, the Greek word for prophets is *prophetes,*
which literally means "to speak forth." From these different Hebrew and Greek words taken together, we gather that a prophet is
one who sees things, that is, who receives revelations, who is in
the service of God, particularly as a messenger, who speaks in his
name. Without receiving, the prophet cannot give, and he cannot
give more than he receives; in fact if he does so, he is a false prophet.

---

[3]George M. Bowman, *The Christ of Hebrews* (Whitby, Ontario: Operation Balance, 2001), 172.

Other Examples of Revelations and Predictions

It is also important to note that a person could receive a revelation and not be a prophet. Abimelech, Pharaoh, and Nebuchadnezzar all received revelations but they were not prophets.

What qualified one to be a prophet was the divine calling, the instruction and the divine commission from God to communicate the divine revelation to others. People do not usually think of Abraham as a prophet but God said "he is a prophet" (Genesis 20:7).

A man could have been a prophet and never predict a thing about the future. Christ said of John the Baptist, "Wherefore went ye out to see a prophet? Yea, I say unto you, and much more than a prophet." Yet the Bible records no predictions made by John the Baptist.

The Samaritan woman at Jacob's well was right when she said of Christ, "Sir, I perceive that thou art a prophet." She said this, not because he had predicted her future, but because he had revealed her past.

The duty of a prophet was to reveal the will of God to the people. This could be done in the form of instruction, admonition and exhortation all of which could be glorious promises or stern rebukes.

Prophets were the ministerial monitors of the people, the interpreters of the law, especially in its moral and spiritual aspects. It was their duty to protest against mere formalism, to stress moral duty, to urge the necessity of godly service, and to promote the interests of truth and righteousness. If the people departed from the path of duty, prophets had to call them back to the law and to the testimony, and to announce the coming terror of the Lord upon the wicked.

The Bible teaches that Christ, the ultimate Prophet whom Moses predicted would come in the future, was already functioning in the Old Testament prophets before his incarnation. Peter wrote about this in 1 Peter 1:10–11:

> Of which salvation the prophets have inquired and searched diligently, who prophesied of the grace that should come unto you, Searching what, or what manner of time the Spirit of Christ who was in them did signify, when he testified beforehand the sufferings of Christ and the glory that should follow.

THE EVIDENCE AND PROOF THAT CHRIST WAS THAT PROPHET

He Taught as One Having Authority

The Old Testament prophet commonly united three methods of fulfilling his office, those of teaching, predicting, and miracle working. In all these respects, Jesus Christ did the work of a prophet. He taught the Word of God. Old Testament prophets, no matter how great, no matter how profound in their speaking or writing, could not match the wisdom and wondrous teaching of the Sermon on the Mount, as found in Matthew 5–7.

His teaching was so great that when he ended his Sermon on the Mount, "the people were astonished at his doctrine; for he taught them as one having authority, and not as the scribes" (Matthew 7:28–29).

He Predicted the Future

His long Olivet discourse in Matthew 24 and 25 has divided sincere Christians into several camps. They call themselves premillennialists, postmillennialists, amillennialists, or preterists, and some humorously call themselves "panmillennialists," because they say, "Everything will pan out all right because Christ is the divine author of Matthew 24 and 25."

Christ Wrought Miracles

Within the two chapters of Matthew 8 and 9, there are at least 10 miracles. You will recall that the feeding of the 5,000 caused the people to say that Jesus was the prophet whose coming was foretold by Moses.

When the Lord Jesus Christ raised to life the dead son of the widow of Nain, it had a tremendous influence upon those who witnessed that miracle. The record says, "And there came fear on

37

all. And they glorified God, saying, A great prophet is raised up among us and God has visited his people" (Luke 7:16).

Consider His Insight

One of the best proofs that Christ was a prophet was the fact that he called himself a prophet. Responding to the Jews who were offended because of his teaching, Jesus said, "A prophet is not without honour, except in his own country, and in his own house" (Matthew 13:57). He also said, "Nevertheless I must walk today and tomorrow, and the day following; for it cannot be that a prophet perish out of Jerusalem" (Luke 13:33).

Imprisoned, John the Baptist sent messengers to ask Christ, "Art thou he that should come, or do we look for another?" (Matthew 11:3). In response, Christ sent them back to John to tell him about the miracles they had seen, and the messages they had heard him preach, and that "the poor have the gospel preached to them" (Matthew 11:4–5).

For further proof of this prophetic office, consider his insight in telling his disciples where they would find a colt for him to ride and what they should tell the owner of the colt. Consider too his telling Peter to get tax money from the mouth of a fish, and how he predicted his own death and resurrection. He even told his apostles about Judas betraying him and how all his disciples would forsake him.

THE FUNCTION OF CHRIST AS THAT PROPHET

The Light of the World

Christ's prophetic work began before he came in the flesh. "That was the true Light," said John, "which lighteth every man that cometh into the world" (John 1:9). All the true light of conscience,

science, philosophy, art and civilization finds it source in Christ whom the Bible says is "the light of the world."

"Our little systems," said Tennyson, "have their day and cease to be; They are but broken lights of you, And you O Lord, art more than they."

All preliminary religious knowledge, whether within or without the bounds of the chosen people, is from Christ, the revealer of God. That is why all of us are wise to heed the warning of Hebrews 12:25, 26:

> See that ye refuse not him that speaketh . . . . whose voice then [at Sinai] shook the earth; but now he hath promised, saying, Yet once more will I make the earth to tremble, not the earth only, but also heaven.

The Prophet Par Excellence

In his earthly ministry, Christ showed himself as the prophet par excellence. While he submitted like the Old Testament prophets to the direction of the Holy Spirit, unlike them, he found the sources of all knowledge and power within himself. The word of God did not come to him; he was the Word.

Christ was described as One who "manifested forth his glory" (John 2:11). Could any of the Old Testament prophets be described like that? Or could any of them have said what Christ said about himself in his short ministry? "Before Abraham was," he said, "I am" (John 8:59). He also said that no man could take his life from him: "I lay it down of myself. I have power to lay it down, and I have power to take it again" (John 10:18).

In his office as prophet, Christ reveals the will of God for our salvation. In other words, he proclaims the gospel. That proclamation was indeed begun by him in Old Testament times, as he sent the Holy Spirit upon the prophets. They testified beforehand of his coming and gave an elementary revelation of the way of salvation.

Teaching of Christ and His Apostles

But when we think of Christ as prophet, we think primarily of the revelation that he gave after he became man. All of his teaching during his earthly ministry is here included. His work as a prophet did not end with his earthly career. Before leaving his disciples, he gave them the promise that the Holy Spirit would be sent to continue the work.

Christ also continued to speak through his apostles. He said, "Settle it therefore in your hearts not to meditate beforehand how to answer: for I will give you a mouth and wisdom, which all of your adversaries shall not be able to withstand or gainsay" (Luke 21:14, 15).

The prophetic work of Christ is also continued down through the ages, as the Holy Spirit enlightens the minds of his people and leads them to understand spiritual truth, which otherwise would be incomprehensible to them. The Bible says that "the natural man receiveth not the things of the Spirit of God: for they are foolishness unto him: neither can he know them, because they are spiritually discerned" (1 Corinthians 2:14).

Since Christ reveals the Father and since the Father is infinite, Christ's prophetic work will be endless. Dr. A. H. Strong, theologian and seminary president, fittingly said:

> In heaven Christ will be the visible God. We shall never see the Father separate from Christ. No man or angel has at any time seen God "whom no man has seen nor can see." The only begotten Son he has declared him, and he will forever declare him.

APPLICATION OF THE OLD TESTAMENT TEXT IN THE NEW TESTAMENT

Stronger than Moses

By the power of the Holy Spirit, Peter applied the prophesy of Moses to Christ. But by changing or adding a few words, his message was stronger than what Moses had said. "And it shall come to pass," said Moses, "that whosoever will not hearken unto my words which he shall speak in my name, I will require it of him."

Peter put it this way: "And it shall come to pass, that every soul, which will not hear that prophet, shall be destroyed from among the people" (Acts 3:23). Moses said the disobedient would be required to give account to the Lord. But Peter said they would be destroyed! Jesus also made remarks that are similar. "If ye believe not that I am he," he said, "ye shall die in your sins" (John 8:24).

That Was Not Enough

The day the Lord Jesus rode into Jerusalem on the back of an ass, the multitudes said, "This is Jesus, the prophet of Nazareth of Galilee."

The day Christ raised the widow's son, the people cried and feared, saying, "A great prophet is raised up among us and God hath visited his people."

Nicodemus said, "Thou art a teacher sent from God."

The woman at the pool in Samaria confessed, "Sir, I perceive that thou art a prophet."

When the people had witnessed the tremendous miracle of Jesus feeding 5,000 persons with five loaves and two fish, they said, "This is of a truth that prophet that should come into the world."

The Jews in the temple at the feast of Tabernacles said, "Of a truth this is the Prophet."

The blind man in John 9, who had just received his sight from Christ, said, "He is a prophet" But that was not enough!

After the Jews had excommunicated and cast the blind man out of the temple, Jesus found him and said, "Dost thou believe on the Son of God?"

Charles Haddon Spurgeon once preached a great sermon on this question asked by Jesus of the former blind man. It was called, "The Question of Questions—Dost Thou Believe On The Son Of God?" In these days of so many counterfeit faiths, it behooves us to examine ourselves to make sure we can answer that question in the manner that the healed blind man answered it. "Lord," he said, "I believe," and he worshiped Christ.

A profession of faith in Christ that is not followed by sincere worship and evidence of holiness in one's life, is a false profession of a counterfeit faith. There is no way that one can say he has been justified who shows no evidence in his life that he has been sanctified, because the two go together like repentance and faith. Faith without repentance is a counterfeit faith.

The reason so many Christians do not strive with all diligence to live in holiness is twofold: First, they do not realize that justification and sanctification are indispensable elements in that plan. This means that it would be impossible to be justified without being sanctified. Because of this, many who profess faith in Christ have a lifestyle not much different from what it was before they professed faith in Christ.

Second, they were not taught or they failed to learn that all believers are called on to "pursue peace with all men, and holiness, without which no man shall see the Lord" (Hebrews 12:14). Though a person is saved by grace alone through faith alone in Christ alone, he is expected to turn from his sins and strive to be as holy as it is possible for a redeemed sinner to be. There is a big need among evangelicals today to understand that genuine faith always leads the believer to surrender his life to Christ and to see himself as a dedicated disciple of Christ. Hymn writer Ray Palmer knew the nature of genuine faith as reflected in these lines:

> *My faith looks up to thee,*
> *Thou Lamb of Calvary,*
> *Saviour Divine:*
> *Now hear me while I pray,*
> *Take all my guilt away,*
> *O let me from this day*
> *Be wholly thine.*

CHAPTER THREE

Why Did Paul the Apostle Suffer So Much?

For he is a chosen vessel unto me, to bear my name before the Gen-
tiles, and kings, and the children of Israel. For I will show him how
great things he must suffer for my name's sake.

(Acts 9:15, 16)

It is the year A.D. 34. A small, bold, arrogant Jew was travel-
ling the dusty road from Jerusalem to Damascus, accompa-
nied by a band of men. He carried with him written authority
from the high priest of Israel to arrest all Christians in Damascus
and take them back to Jerusalem. Suddenly the Jew, whose name
was Saul of Tarsus, was knocked to the ground with a blinding
light. When he rose he was blind, and he had to be led by his
companions to the house of Judas in Damascus, who lived on a
street called Straight.

Things He Must Suffer

Three days later God sent a Christian by the name of Ananias
to Judas's house to give Saul (the man who had been breathing out
threatenings and slaughter against Christians) his eyesight. "For I
will show him," said God, "how great things he must suffer for my
name's sake" (Acts 9:16).

Twenty-seven years later, in A.D. 61, Saul of Tarsus, now known as Paul the apostle of the Lord Jesus Christ, was sitting in Philippi writing these words to the Christian church located in the city of Corinth:

Are they ministers of Christ? (I speak as a fool) I am more; in labours more abundant, in stripes above measure, in prisons more frequent, in deaths oft. Of the Jews five times received I forty stripes save one. Thrice was I beaten with rods, once was I stoned, thrice I suffered shipwreck, a night and a day I have been in the deep;

In journeyings often, in perils of water, in perils of robbers, in perils by my own countrymen, in perils by the heathen, in perils in the city, in perils in the wilderness, in perils in the sea, in perils among false brethren; in weariness and painfulness, in watchings often, in hunger and thirst, in fastings often, in cold and nakedness.

Beside those things that are without, that which cometh upon me daily, the care of all the churches . . . . In Damascus the governor under Aretas the king kept the city of the Damascenes with a garrison, desirous to apprehend me: and through a window in a basket was I let down by the wall, and escaped his hands.
(2 Corinthians 11:23–28, 32–33)

Why did the apostle Paul suffer so much in fulfillment of the prophecy of God, which we have read in Acts 9:16? All the apostles suffered. History records their martyrdom, except John the apostle who was banished to the isle of Patmos, but none suffered like the apostle Paul. Why? Paul suffered so much because he was God's chosen vessel to destroy Judaism and set up the new revelation of Christianity.

Christianity and Judaism

Someone is sure to say, "I thought Christianity was the fulfillment or the outgrowth of the Old Testament religion."

That is what a Christian will answer, but has an unsaved Jew, a Moslem, a Hindu, or a Buddhist ever believed that?

Someone else raises their voice and says, "We are living in the twenty-first century, and Judaism is still with us today. We have Jewish colleges and synagogues, and Jews still celebrate the Passover and many other Jewish customs."

Today's Judaism is not even a shadow of the Old Testament religion. The Jewish temple is gone, the Jewish system of priests and temple and tabernacle helpers (the whole tribe of Levi) ordained by God are gone, and more importantly, all animal sacrifices are gone. Since A.D. 70 when the Roman army destroyed the temple, killed over one million Jews in the leveling of Jerusalem and sent thousands into captivity, Old Testament Judaism ceased to be.

Dogmatically Exclusive

Most people in the world—even most Christians—do not realize how dogmatically exclusive New Testament Christianity is. Listen to just two verses. Acts 4:12 says, "Neither is there salvation in any other: for there is none other name [except Jesus] under heaven given among men, whereby we must be saved." In John 8:24, Jesus said, "For if ye believe not that I am he, ye shall die in your sins."

Millions of people in this world have religion, but comparatively few have salvation purchased by the shed blood of Jesus Christ. Therefore, they do not have his gift of the Holy Spirit living within, bearing witness that they are children of God. Paul seemed to believe that Judaism was no longer God's religion for he called it the Jews' religion:

> For ye have heard of my way of life in time past in the Jews' religion, how that beyond measure I persecuted the church of God, and wasted it: and profited in the Jews' religion above many

my equals in mine own nation, being more exceedingly zealous of the traditions of my fathers.

(Galatians 1:13–14)

180 Degree Change in Direction

It has been said that when a man is regenerated, he changes the direction of his life 180 degrees. He has a new desire to go in a direction completely opposite to the way he used to travel. Certainly that was true in the life of Saul of Tarsus. After his encounter with the living Christ, his Pharisaical prejudices and traditions were replaced with spiritual insights, and he used his zeal for the cause of Christ. He preached the faith that he formerly sought to destroy, and God made the astonishing revelation to him that believers in Christ are "Abraham's seed, and heirs according to the promise."

That and other revelations from the Lord changed Paul from being the persecutor to being the persecuted. Instead of the hunter, he became the hunted. He was totally committed to the risen Christ and his church—known as the body of Jesus Christ. He abandoned the hopeless, nationalistic expectations of Old Testament Israel and preached salvation, not by the Jewish race, but by God's sovereign grace.

That change in his doctrine made him the target of zealous Jews with whose religion and ideas he formerly agreed. Outraged by what they thought was his betrayal of the "true" religion, they followed him from town to town. They stirred up both Jews and Gentiles against him and frequently had him imprisoned, whipped, and beaten. On one occasion they stoned him and left him for dead (Acts 14:19).

Their cruel and wicked and constant persecution did not prevent him from exposing their false doctrine. In his epistles to the first-century churches, Paul said again and again that the Jews were wrong. He pointed out that they were not God's chosen people. Only those of every race who were spiritually born from above were the legitimate people of God.

The name of Saul of Tarsus was changed to Paul the apostle. And God's redemptive focus was changed from one small nation in the Middle East to a world-wide body of people drawn from "all nations, and kindreds, and people, and tongues" (Revelation 7:9). What a shock to Paul, Peter, John and other first-century Jews to discover that it had always been God's intention to expand his salvation from the little nation of Israel to the whole world! Paul called the revelation of Gentiles receiving God's salvation, "the mystery of Christ." In Ephesians 3, he went on to show how the Lord made the new revelation known unto him and other apostles and prophets.

What a Dilemma for the Jews!

This one worldwide body of believers was the "one body" of Christ (Ephesians 2:16). Only Gentiles and Jews who believed in Christ were to be heirs of God's promises. What place of relationship with God did that leave for the nation of Israel? Paul said it was finished because the family or household of God now contained both Gentiles and Jews who exercised true repentance and genuine faith in Christ.

Those who were citizens of the Israel of old, but who had not received Christ, were simply unsaved members of one of the many nations of the world. Paul makes this clear in Romans 9:6. "For they are not all Israel," he said, "who are of Israel." Those who refused to repent and believe in Jesus Christ as the Messiah and Saviour were not saved. They were merely racial Israelites or "Israel after the flesh" (1 Corinthians 10:18).

When Paul said that only Jews who believed in the Lord Jesus Christ were the true Israel of God, it infuriated the Jews, who increased their opposition across the Roman Empire. His former colleagues among the Pharisees, the Sadducees, and the rest of the unbelieving Jews, intensified their efforts to silence him. It was bad enough that such an eminent member of the Pharisees had received Jesus of Nazareth as the long, promised Messiah. But it was much worse that he now went about saying that the body of Jews and Gentiles who believed in that Messiah had replaced the nation of Israel as God's chosen people.

Jewish Provincialism Destroyed

It was perfectly natural for the Pharisees, chief priests, elders, and Sadducees to attack Paul and the other apostles so violently. The revelation God gave the early church made it clear that the nation of Israel had lost what it perceived to be its monopoly on God. With their religious traditions, personal prejudices, and nationalistic expectations proved to be obsolete by the gospel of God's grace, it was inevitable that the Jewish leaders would react with great ferocity. In fact, their anger against Christ, his gospel and his people knew no bounds.

For 2000 years there was a great difference between the nation of Israel and the other nations of the world. God had set Israel apart by blessing them more than any other nation. But just as the birth of Christ divides time into B.C. and A.D., so Calvary destroyed the provincialism of Judaism with the universality of Christianity.

Before his conversion to Christ, Saul of Tarsus was a proud Pharisee who believed beyond all shadow of doubt that the Jewish race was something special among the nations in the sight of God. As Paul the apostle of Jesus Christ who had received special revelations of truth from the Lord, he was compelled to cast off what he formerly believed and to call himself "the Apostle to the Gentiles."

The Pharisees' Five Basic Beliefs

Like his fellow Pharisees, Saul of Tarsus used to boast about these five basic beliefs: (1) The importance of the law, (2) the necessity for circumcision, (3) their natural descent from Abraham, (4) their assurance that their race would be restored to a powerful national kingdom, such as that under David and his son Solomon, and (5) their unabated hatred for Gentiles. Consider how Paul, the apostle of Christ to the Gentiles, destroyed or changed every one of these five basic beliefs or positions.

THE LAW WAS THE FOUNDATION OF JUDAISM

The law given to Moses on Mount Sinai was the foundation of Judaism. It was in three divisions: the Commandments, the judgments and the ordinances. Think how sacred the Ten Commandments were to Jews especially when they knew that God had written them with his finger on the tables of stone!

Justification by Law Impossible

The Jews for centuries had broken the law, misunderstood the purpose of the law, and thought it was necessary to keep the law in order to be right with God. Fifteen hundred years after the law had been given, Paul the apostle reminded the Jews that God gave the law to Moses about 500 years after his covenant with Abraham. He also said the law was merely a temporary instrument and that it could not make men right with God,

"But that no man is justified by the law in the sight of God, it is evident," he said, "for the just shall live by faith, and the law is not of faith" (Galatians 3:11–12).

Like his master, the Lord Jesus, who said that "he came not to destroy the Law," Paul was careful to remind the Jews that the law was holy, spiritual, and good. The law, he said, was not made for a righteous man. He kept reminding the Jews that they could not be saved by keeping the law.

The Law Was Set Aside

Boasting, he said, was excluded, not by the "law of works" but by "the law of faith" (Romans 3:27). Christ brought something in the new covenant of the gospel that was alien to the Jews' way of thinking. Paul called it "the law of the Spirit of life in Christ Jesus" (Romans 8:2). He also presented the argument that love would never do anyone wrong. "Therefore love," he said, "is the fulfilling of the Law" (Romans 13:10).

Imagine how a Jew steeped in religious traditions and Pharisaical prejudice and hatred for Gentiles would receive these words from the Bible: "The former commandment is set aside because it was weak and useless for the law made nothing perfect" (Hebrews 7:18–19).

Paul made a similar statement when he wrote, "For what the law could not do, in that it was weak through the flesh, God sending his own Son in the likeness of sinful flesh, and for sin, condemned sin in the flesh, that the righteousness of the law might be fulfilled in us, who walk not after the flesh, but after the Spirit" (Romans 8:3–4).

Imagine telling Jews, whether Pharisees or Sadducees or priests or elders or scribes, that the law was weak and that it couldn't make anyone perfect. No wonder that they beat, stoned, and tried to kill Paul.

CIRCUMCISION WAS THE SIGN OF THE ABRAHAMIC COVENANT

Demanded by Law

On the eighth day after his birth, every Jewish boy was circumcised. This means that men like Isaac, Jacob, his 12 sons, Moses, Joshua, David, Solomon, Isaiah, Jeremiah, Daniel, Jesus, Paul, John, Peter, John Mark, Matthew, and James, were circumcised eight days after they were born.

Scriptures plainly teach that circumcision, as far as Abraham and the Jews after him were concerned, was a sign of the covenant that God had made with Abraham. A man could not partake of the Passover, the most important feast in the Jewish community, unless he was circumcised. The Jews even had a saying, "A circumcised beggar was nearer to God than an uncircumcised king."

The Jews had their Old Testament, and they knew from the book of Exodus that God almost killed their great leader Moses, because he had not circumcised his two sons born of a Gentile wife (Exodus 4). They also knew that God had demanded that before the male Israelites (who had been born in the wilderness, but not circumcised) could enter the Promised Land, they had to be circumcised.

Paul's Strange Statements

Two thousand years after God's covenant with Abraham and ultimately the nation of Israel—with its sign of male circumcision—Paul began his ministry. Though perceived by the Pharisees to be a renegade Jew, because he had acknowledged a crucified Nazarene as the Messiah, he made these strange statements:

> Is any man called being circumcised? let him not become uncircumcised. Is any called in uncircumcision? let him not be circumcised. Circumcision is nothing, and uncircumcision is nothing, but the keeping of the commandments of God.
>
> (1 Corinthians 7:18, 19)

> For in Jesus Christ neither circumcision avails any thing, nor uncircumcision: but faith which works by love.
>
> (Galatians 5:6)

> For neither they themselves who are circumcised keep the law; but desire to have you circumcised, that they may glory in your flesh.
>
> (Galatians 6:13)

> For in Christ Jesus neither circumcision avails any thing, nor uncircumcision, but a new creation.
>
> (Galatians 5:6)

> For we are the circumcision who worship God, in the spirit, and rejoice in Christ Jesus and have no confidence in the flesh.
>
> (Philippians 3:3)

Ye are complete in Christ, in whom also ye are circumcised with the circumcision made without hands, in putting off the body of sins of the flesh by the circumcision of Christ.

(Colossians 2:11)

Neither is that circumcision, which is outward in the flesh: But he is a Jew, which is one inwardly; and circumcision is that of the heart.

(Romans 2:28–29)

Jews believed that circumcision was not only important to their religion, but it was indispensable to being right with God. Imagine them being told that circumcision availed nothing! And it was like rubbing salt in their religious wounds for Paul to say that uncircumcised Gentiles were complete in Christ. They had a circumcision made without hands because God had circumcised their hearts by a new spiritual birth from above! Is it any wonder that Jews tried again and again to kill Paul?

NATIONALITY OR DESCENT FROM ABRAHAM

Nationalistic Pride

Because of their history as descendants of Abraham, Jews were filled with nationalistic pride. It is one thing to be a good citizen with a sense of sincere patriotism. It is something else again to let nationalistic pride blind you to the truth. That was the reason that John the Baptist had warned the Pharisees and Sadducees about their racial pride.

"O generation of vipers," he said to them, "who hath warned you to flee from the wrath to come? Bring forth therefore fruits meet for repentance: And think not to say within yourselves, 'We have Abraham to our father:' for I say to you, that God is able of these stones to raise up children unto Abraham" (Matthew 3:7–9).

This Did Not Abraham

A few months later, the Lord Jesus uttered stronger words on this same subject. To the Jews who said they were Abraham's children, Jesus said, "If ye were Abraham's children, ye would do the works of Abraham. But now ye seek to kill me, a man that hath told you the truth, which I have heard of God: this did not Abraham . . . . Ye are of your father the devil" (John 8:39, 40, 44).

Herod beheaded John the Baptist, and the Jews had Christ crucified for making such statements. Therefore it should not surprise anyone that the Jews made many attempts on the life of Paul when he spoke and wrote as he did. For example, in his epistle to the Romans, he wrote, "For he is not a Jew which is one outwardly; neither is that circumcision, which is outward in the flesh: But he is a Jew, which is one inwardly: and circumcision is that of the heart, in the spirit and not in the letter, whose praise is not of men but of God" (2:28–29).

A Hopeless Search

In Galatians 6, Paul said that the Gentiles were the true Israel of God because they were saved. No wonder Jews tried to stone him to death at Lystra! Paul did not remove the law, circumcision, and nationalistic pride just to be malicious. He was making an important point both for believers, so they could understand who they really were, and for the Jewish people (whom he really loved) so they would not be deceived into a hopeless search for salvation because of their identification with God's law, their circumcision, the sign of the Abrahamic covenant, and racial ancestry.

THE KINGDOM

Not Their Kind of Kingdom

Both John the Baptist and the Lord Jesus Christ began their ministry in the same way. Their message was, "Repent for the kingdom of heaven is at hand" (Matthew 3:2, Mark 1:15). The Jews did not repent as a nation because John the Baptist and the Lord Jesus Christ did not preach the kind of kingdom the Jews wanted.

They wanted the glory of an earthly kingdom led by a Messiah who would deliver them from the power of the Roman Empire and rule a restored Jewish nation. They had their visionary thoughts on the past and the glorious and triumphant reigns of David and his son Solomon. John the Baptist and Jesus Christ, however, were not materialists or worldly nationalists. Instead, they preached about the invisible, spiritual kingdom of almighty God.

Their message did not go down with the Jews because they were so self-centered and arrogant about their own ideas that they could not accept it. Nevertheless, what John the Baptist and Jesus preached fulfilled Old Testament prophecy because they preached the Word of God.

Here's the Evidence

God promised that the seed of David would "build a house for my name, and I will establish the throne of his kingdom forever" (2 Samuel 7:13). The natural fulfillment of that promise came about when David's son Solomon built the first temple of Israel. Disobedience, however, caused Solomon's temple, throne, and kingdom to crumble and disappear rather than survive forever. The complete fulfillment of the promise to David occurred after Christ's death, resurrection, and ascension.

The kingdom of God is not a natural, earthly, political kingdom that will be established at some uncertain date in a little country on the eastern shore of the Mediterranean Sea. It is a present, eternal, universal, immovable, and spiritual kingdom. Taken in its proper context, the Greek word *basileia*, translated "kingdom" in the English New Testament, does not mean a physical kingdom with a specific and limited location; it means the universal, spiritual, unchangeable, and sovereign authority of God.

Christ resisted the efforts of people in his own day to make him a natural king like David or Solomon. He had just supernaturally fed 5000 people with five loaves and two fish, and they were looking to make him their bread-and-fish king. Referring to Jesus, the Bible says, "When he perceived that they would come and take him by force, to make him a king, he departed again into a mountain himself alone" (John 6:15).

What Christ Said about His Kingdom

There was no question as to the nature of the kingdom described by Jesus Christ. It was an invisible, spiritual kingdom. Listen to what he said about the kingdom during his earthly ministry:

- "But I tell you of a truth, there be some standing here, which shall not taste of death, till they see the kingdom of God" (Luke 9:27). He was speaking of the soon coming judgment of the Jewish nation, which would be so devastating that only a fool would deny it was a fulfillment of what Jesus had said.
- "The kingdom of God comes not with observation . . . . for, behold, the kingdom of God is within you" (Luke 17:20–21). This shows that God's kingdom is an invisible spirit kingdom and not a material or national kingdom.
- "My kingdom is not of this world; if my kingdom were of this world, then would my servants fight, that I should not be delivered to the Jews" (John 18:36). Another proof that the kingdom of God is not one to be defended by military force because its very nature is not of this world.
- "Except a man be born again, he cannot see the kingdom of God . . . . Except a man be born of water and the Spirit, he cannot enter into the kingdom of God" (John 3:3, 5). These words of Jesus show that one had to be spiritually born and given new spiritual life to enable him to become a citizen of the kingdom of God.

Promise to David Fulfilled in Christ's Resurrection

The angel Gabriel told Mary that God would give her son Jesus "the throne of his father David" (Luke 1:32). On the day of

Pentecost, Peter confirmed that God had done exactly that. In his sermon to the Jews gathered in Jerusalem, he said that when God promised David that "he would raise up Christ to sit on his throne; he seeing this before spoke of the resurrection of Christ . . . . This Jesus has God raised up whereof we all are witnesses . . . . being by the right hand of God exalted" (Acts 2:30–33).

As one would expect, when Christ, the greater David, rose triumphantly from the dead and ascended to heaven, he took his place on a greater throne than the throne of David. The throne of David was but an Old Testament type of the spiritual throne of Christ.

The Stone Cut Without Hands

The four kingdoms represented by the image in Nebuchadnezzar's dream (Daniel 2:28–42) were Babylon, Medo-Persia, Greece, and Rome. The fifth kingdom, "the stone cut without hands" in Daniel 2:34 was the kingdom of "the God of heaven" (Daniel 2:44).

In interpreting the dream, Daniel said that the latter kingdom was not to be set up at some date which is yet future from our time now, but that it would appear or be manifested in the days of the other kingdoms (Daniel 2:44). That means it had to appear, and did appear, before the fall of the Roman Empire, which occurred more than 1500 years ago.

Delivered from the Power of Darkness

Paul taught exactly what John the Baptist, Christ, and Peter taught about the kingdom. "For the kingdom of God is not meat and drink," he said, "but righteousness and peace and joy in the Holy Spirit" (Romans 14:17).

He also said "that flesh and blood cannot inherit the kingdom of God" (1 Corinthians 15:50). Speaking of himself and his readers, he wrote that God "hath delivered us from the power of darkness, and hath translated us into the kingdom of his dear son: in whom we have redemption through his blood, even the forgiveness of sins" (Colossians 1:13).

Luke frequently reported in Acts that Paul preached a spiritual kingdom in the cities of Asia Minor such as Lystra, Iconium, Antioch, and Ephesus. He took his kingdom message into Macedonia and Greece and ultimately to the capital of the Roman Empire. Tradition says he also preached the gospel of the kingdom in Spain. Though the world around him was pagan and immoral, and Judaea was soon to be shaken by war, he never wavered in his belief in a kingdom that was established forever.

The writer to the Hebrews felt the same way. "Wherefore," he said, "we receive a kingdom which cannot be moved" (Hebrews 12:28). No national or physical kingdom can be described in that manner. A kingdom that cannot be moved has to be a spiritual kingdom. What were Paul and the other apostles really doing by preaching and writing so much about the kingdom of God? They were demolishing the Jewish hope and belief in a future restoration of a physical kingdom such as David had.

WHY THE JEWS HATED GENTILES

They Even Hated Half-Jews

Most Jews hated Gentiles. They had good reason not to be in love with the *Goi* or Gentiles. They had a history of harassment from Gentile nations. Early in their history, Egypt enslaved them for hundreds of years. After they established themselves in Canaan, neighboring nations kept attacking them.

It was a major part of their story that they were attacked, captured, harassed, carried away, overrun and often killed by Philistines, Midianites, Hittites, Ammonites, Moabities, Syrians, Assyrians, Medo-Persians, Greeks, Babylonians, Romans and other foreigners.

The Jews had such nationalistic pride that they did not even accept half-Jews such as the Samaritans. That is the reason the Lord Jesus gave us the parable of the Good Samaritan (Luke 10). The Samaritan woman of John 4 even asked the question of Christ, "How is it that thou, being a Jew, asketh drink from me, a woman of

Samaria?" And Christ's own disciples marveled that he talked with this woman when they came back to him from buying meat in the city. At that time, the Jews had no dealings with the Samaritans.

A Light of the Gentiles

The apostles and brethren were shocked when they heard that the Gentiles had received the Word of God. When Peter came back from the house of Cornelius, the centurion in Caesarea, we are told that the Jews contended with him (Acts 11:2).

Although the first part of the book of Acts deals mostly with Peter, it was Paul who was the missionary and gospel preacher to, and the church founder among, the Gentiles. In Acts 13, after being persecuted by the Jews, in Antioch in Pisidia Paul and Barnabas spoke to them and said, "It was necessary that the word of God should first have been spoken to you: but seeing ye put it from you, and judge yourselves unworthy of everlasting life, lo, we turn to the Gentiles. For so hath the Lord commanded us, saying, 'I have set thee to be a light of the Gentiles, that thou shouldest be for salvation unto the ends of the earth'" (Acts 13:46–47).

After Paul preached Christ to the Jews in Corinth, the Jews blasphemed, and Luke records Paul saying, "Your blood be upon your own heads: I am clean: from henceforth I will go to the Gentiles" (Acts 18:6).

Wrath to the Uttermost

There are a couple of verses in 1 Thessalonians that dispensationalists seem to ignore in their attempts to interpret them. Speaking to believers about persecution, Paul said, "Ye also suffered like things of your own countrymen, even as they have of the Jews: who both killed the Lord Jesus, and their own prophets, and have persecuted us; and they please not God, and are contrary to all men: Forbidding us to speak to the Gentiles that they might be saved, to fill up their sins always for the wrath is come upon them to the uttermost" (1 Thessalonians 2:14–16).

Does divine wrath "to the uttermost" sound as though God was going to arrange for their return to their home in Palestine and for a rebuilding of the temple that was destroyed in A.D. 70? Paul was speaking of the utter destruction of the Jewish nation and its apostate religion.

Do We Appreciate the Difference?

In Romans 11:13 Paul wrote, "For I speak to you Gentiles, inasmuch as I am the apostle of the Gentiles, I magnify my office." The Jews never forgave him for that position; this was another reason why he suffered so much and why he was a target for their hatred and persecution.

I do not think that we Christians of today appreciate enough what it cost Paul, Peter, the other apostles, and many other first-century Jews to forsake Judaism and receive Jesus Christ as Saviour. The destruction, replacement, and supplanting of Old Testament Judaism that the apostles preached was confirmed by God in A.D. 70 when Christ used the Roman army under Titus to destroy Jerusalem and its magnificent temple.

Some Christians believe we should celebrate that date as we observe Christmas and Easter. Why do they think that way? Perhaps it is because we rarely if ever thank God for the convenience of New Testament Christianity as compared with Old Testament Judaism.

Instead of having to go to a certain place to worship, we are beneficiaries of what Jesus said to the woman at the well: "The hour cometh, and now is, when the true worshipers shall worship the Father in spirit and in truth" (John 4:23). There is such a penchant for unbiblical methods for worship today, that we do well when we go to a worship service at the local church to pray and ask God to move the hearts of all who attend to worship him in spirit and in truth.[4]

---

[4]For more on worship, see the book, *Whatever Happened to Christian Worship?* by George M. Bowman.

Instead of going to a priest, we have our Lord Jesus Christ, a priest forever after the order of Melchizedek. Instead of having to kill a lamb, a goat, a bullock or turtle dove, all animal sacrifices ended when the Lamb of God cried from the cross, "It is finished." The question is, do we appreciate the difference?

Today, thousands of Christians are being persecuted. It was recently reported that more than 60 countries presently harass, persecute, torture, and, in some cases, kill Christians because of their profession of faith in Jesus Christ. Many of those under persecution take comfort from the last thing that Paul wrote: "Yea, and all that will live godly in Christ Jesus shall suffer persecution" (2 Timothy 3:12). Thank God that Paul was willing to suffer for the cause of our Lord and Saviour Jesus Christ!

CHAPTER FOUR

DOES THE BIBLE TEACH A FREE OFFER OF THE GOSPEL?

Moreover, brethren, I declare unto you the gospel which I preached unto you, which also ye have received, and wherein ye stand; . . . For I delivered unto you first of all that which I also received, how that Christ died for our sins according to the scriptures; And that he was buried, and that he rose again the third day according to the scriptures.

(1 Corinthians 15:1–4)

If there is one chapter in the Bible that unsaved, ungodly people, as well as a host of Arminian believers, were permitted to eliminate from Holy Writ, it would be the ninth chapter of Paul's epistle to the Romans. This important chapter has much to say about God's sovereignty, severity, election, and reprobation.

It is so strong that even Paul asks the question, "Is there unrighteousness with God?" Later on he even rebukes anyone who, reading the chapter, dares to question what Paul has written. "Who art thou," he asks, "that repliest against God?" The theology and statements in Romans 9 are so deep and thought-provoking that the average reader forgets how Paul introduced the subject of that chapter. In that introduction, he makes one of the most remarkable statements in the entire Bible. He said,

I say the truth in Christ, I lie not, my conscience also bearing me witness in the Holy Spirit, that I have great heaviness and continual sorrow in my heart. For I could wish that I myself were accursed from Christ for my brethren, my kinsmen, according to the flesh.

(Romans 9:1–3)

Then after his arguments for the sovereignty of God in all things, he writes, "Brethren, my heart's desire and prayer to God for Israel is, that they might be saved" (Romans 10:1). Some might wonder if Paul was sincere. Here he has a kind of theological sandwich: an argument for sovereign election in the salvation of sinners tucked in between two expressions of desire for the salvation of Jewish sinners.

Is it theologically sound for an expression of desire and prayer for a people to be saved to immediately precede and follow statements about God's sovereign election and retribution? Those statements include:

- Salvation is not of man's will or works, but of God who shows mercy.
- God having mercy on some and hardening the rest.
- Vessels of mercy prepared for glory and vessels of wrath fitted to destruction.

Some charge Paul with inconsistency because he said he wished he could be accursed from Christ that his Jewish brethren might be saved, and then argued that sinners were saved exclusively by God's election and mercy.

That Paul was sincere in his desire for Jews to be saved can be seen in the fact that in every city he visited, he went to the synagogue and preached the gospel first to the Jews. Though he believed and taught the doctrines of sovereign grace in the salvation of sinners, he also believed and taught that the gospel of God's grace was to be freely offered to all men—both Jews and Gentiles.

For example, examine what he said in his sermon on Mars Hill in Athens. Preaching to pagan Greek philosophers, he told them that worshiping idols made by man was not a thinking man's religion. He told them that in the past, God overlooked their pagan idolatry. Then he said that God "commandeth all men everywhere to repent" (Acts 17:30).

Since Paul has been proved to be a man of sincerity and integrity, he must have meant what he said. And this in spite of what he wrote in Romans 11:7: "Israel hath not obtained that which he seeketh for," he wrote, "but the election hath obtained it, and the rest were blinded."

When some hear about the doctrine of unconditional election of some to salvation, they ask, "Why preach the gospel to every creature if God the Father has chosen only a limited number to be saved?" Unable to answer such a question, many preachers and evangelists have begun using this false appeal to sinners: "God wants to save you, but he cannot do so unless you give him your permission."

Speak to others about the biblical doctrine of the atonement which says Jesus died only for those whom God chose and gave to him, and they will ask, "If God the Son died to effect the salvation of only those chosen and given to him by the Father, then what is the use of giving the Gospel to the world at large?" Even some preachers find it difficult to reconcile the truth that Jesus died to save only his elect people with the truth that the gospel is to be preached to all.

When others hear that the new birth is an independent, sovereign, and exclusive work of the Holy Spirit on the elect only, with which man has nothing to do, they ask, "Where is the propriety in telling sinners that whosoever believeth in Christ shall not perish but have everlasting life?" Unable to answer such a question, most of today's evangelists have turned to decision and invitational evangelism that says, in effect, that a sinner's salvation depends upon what he does.

As we seek to answer these questions we will also find how to resolve the seeming paradox between God's sovereign grace in the salvation of sinners, and his command to preach the gospel to every creature. If you desire to be better informed about the resolution of this seeming paradox, consider the answers given in this chapter to these three questions: First, what is the nature of the gospel? Second, is the biblical offer of the gospel a free offer? And third, is the free offer of the gospel sincerely made?

WHAT IS THE NATURE OF THE GOSPEL?

Concerning His Son

Modern evangelists often present the gospel as though its major element is concern for sinners. They say, "God loves you and wants to save you." They often speak of what the sinner is supposed to receive by making a decision for Christ. Some offer healing miracles, the restoration of broken marriages, financial and career success, and many other goodies of what they call the abundant life.

When we study the Bible, however, we find that the gospel is God's good news, not concerning sinners, but concerning the Lord Jesus Christ. It is true that the gospel is directed toward sinners, but the subject of the gospel is the Lord Jesus Christ. In Romans, the clearest explanation of salvation by grace and justification through faith, Paul said that he was "called to be an apostle, separated unto the gospel of God . . . concerning his Son, Jesus Christ our Lord" (Romans 1:1, 3).

A Gospel Summation

In his summary description of the gospel, Paul said, "Moreover, brethren, I declare unto you the gospel which I preached unto you, which also ye have received, and wherein ye stand; by which also ye are saved, if ye keep in memory what I preached unto you, unless you have believed in vain.

"For I delivered unto you first of all that which I also received, how that Christ died for our sins according to the scriptures; and that he was buried, and that he rose again the third day according to the scriptures" (1 Corinthians 15:1–4).

Notice that the gospel is about the death, burial and resurrection of Jesus Christ. It is about Jesus who "became obedient unto death, even the death of the cross" (Philippians 2:8). To preach the gospel, then is to maintain a universal testimony to the matchless worth of the person and work of the Lord Jesus Christ.

Evangelistic Triumph Assured

One who sincerely preaches the apostolic gospel of Christ cannot help but triumph in his ministry, because God uses the gospel to save some and to condemn others. Paul explained this in 2 Corinthians 2:14–16:

> Now thanks be unto God, who always causes us to triumph in Christ, and makes manifest the savour of his knowledge by us in every place. For we are unto God a sweet savour of Christ, in them that are saved, and in them that perish: To the one we are the savour of death unto death; and to the other the savor of life unto life. And who is sufficient for these things?

To have such triumph, however, one must be careful to preach the genuine gospel because since the apostolic age several perversions of the gospel have appeared. They range from the "gospel" of works to a "gospel" that offers a mixture of grace and works. The gospel is not an "offer" to be bandied about by evangelistic peddlers, with the results depending upon the success of the evangelist's invitational appeal and whether a sinner will let Jesus come into his heart.

The gospel is no mere invitation, but a proclamation concerning Christ, which is true whether men believe it or not. No man is asked to believe that Christ died for him in particular. The gospel in brief, is this: Christ died for sinners, you are a sinner, believe in Christ and you shall be saved. In the gospel, God simply announces the means by which men may be saved.

Those means are the exercise of sincere repentance from sin and the exercise of genuine faith in Jesus Christ. The gospel commands all men to repent and believe, and those who do will be saved.

Why a Universal Offer?

Before Christ returned to heaven, he said that repentance and remission of sins were to be preached in his name "unto all the nations" (Luke 24:47). Why? Because God's elect are scattered abroad among all nations, and it is by the preaching and hearing of the gospel that they are called out of the world. The gospel is the means that God uses in the saving of his chosen ones.

By nature, God's elect are children of wrath "even as others." They are lost sinners who need to be saved, and apart from Christ, there is no salvation for them. Hence, the gospel must be believed by them before they can rejoice in the knowledge of sins forgiven. "The Gospel," said Arthur Pink, "is God's winnowing fan: it separates the chaff from the wheat and gathers the latter into his garner."

There are other purposes for the gospel besides the calling out of the elect. Just as the sun shines whether blind men see it or not, and the rain falls upon rocky mountains and desert wastes as well as fruitful valleys, so also the gospel falls upon the ears of the non-elect.

The power of the gospel is one of God's agencies for holding in check the wickedness of the world. Many who are never saved by the gospel are reformed, their lusts bridled, and they are restrained from becoming worse. The gospel in many instances is a test of character. It demonstrates that men are at enmity against God: the rejection of the gospel justifies the description of men given by the Lord Jesus. "Men," he said, "loved darkness rather than light, because their deeds were evil" (John 3:19).

IS THE BIBLICAL OFFER
OF THE GOSPEL A FREE OFFER?

The Confessions of Faith

"God invites all indiscriminately by outward preaching," said John Calvin, "and in this invitation is the grace of God offered unto us . . . . The mercy of God is offered equally to those who believe and to those who believe not."

The confessions of faith written by Protestant Reformers endorse this position. The Westminster Confession of Faith of the Presbyterian Church says, "God freely offereth unto sinners life and salvation by Jesus Christ, requiring of them faith in him that they may be saved."

The Baptist New Hampshire Confession of Faith has a whole section entitled "The Freeness of Salvation" which reads, "We believe that the blessings of salvation are made free to all by the gospel; that it is the immediate duty of all to accept them by a cordial penitent and obedient faith; and that nothing prevents the salvation of the greatest sinner on earth, but his own inherent depravity and voluntary rejection of the gospel; which rejection involves him in aggravated condemnation."

Unscriptural and Harmful

Some hyper-Calvinists say that there is no need for a universal call even outwardly to sinners and that a call should be given only to a conscious sinner. Only the convicted and contrite who possess the inward marks should be called because only they have the right to come to Christ.

This restricted presentation of the gospel is not only unscriptural, but practically harmful. It causes the sinner to search continually within to see whether he or she is under conviction, instead of heeding the divine command and promise. This leads to the confusion of many who wonder whether they have been called. What do the following verses mean if each of them is not a universal call?

"Ho, every one that thirsteth, come to the waters, and he that hath no money; come, buy and eat; yea, come, buy wine and milk without money and without price" (Isaiah 55:1).

"And the Spirit and the bride say, Come. And let him that heareth say, Come. And let him that is athirst come. And whosoever will, let him take the water of life freely" (Revelation 22:17).

"Come unto me, all ye that labour and are heavy laden, and I will give you rest" (Matthew 11:28).

Arminianism and Calvinism

God is not offering something that he is unwilling to bestow. God offers Christ cordially and affectionately in the gospel; his very heart goes out after sinners in the call and offer of it. It is not possible to conceive anything more affectionate than the words in which God speaks to sinners in Isaiah 55, Ezekiel 33, and Hosea 11. God's whole heart and soul is in the offer and promise of the gospel.

Someone objects, "So few really believe, and God has to give the elect an effectual call." That is correct, but that does not change the sincerity of the universal call. Arminian theology believes the universal offer of salvation includes a declaration that Christ made atonement for every man and that God intends to save each one if man will let him.

Calvinists affirm that while the Gospel offer expresses God's revealed purpose to save all who believe on his Son, it does not express God's unrevealed and sovereign will as it relates to election and the extent of the atonement. Although God's secret will regulates all his dispensations toward his creatures, it forms no part of the rule either of our faith or of our duty. The unconverted are not called upon to believe that they are elected or that Christ died for them in particular.

Ralph Erskine, an old Scottish preacher, rightly said, "Let Arminians maintain at their peril their universal redemption, but we must maintain at our peril the universal offer."

We should not be worried about the consistency of our position as long as it is scriptural. It is not always necessary to satisfy human reason. God commands us to obey his Word, and that is what we should do.

When God ordered Abraham to offer up Isaac, Abraham might have said, "No, it is not consistent with thy statement, 'In Isaac shall thy seed be called.'" Instead of arguing with God's command, Abraham obeyed the Lord.

Jeremiah might have refused to preach because God's command to preach sounded like it was contradictory. "Therefore," said the Lord, "thou shalt speak all these words unto them; but they will not hearken to thee: thou shalt also call unto them; but they will not answer thee" (Jeremiah 7:27). Jeremiah, however, did not question the Lord's word: He obeyed him.

Ezekiel could have felt the same way—that the Lord's command for him to preach to the house of Israel, knowing that the people would not hearken to him, sounded contradictory (Ezekiel 3:4, 7). Instead of trying to understand or find a reason for the Lord giving such a strange command, Ezekiel knew the Lord and that it was right to obey him.

IS THE FREE OFFER OF THE GOSPEL SINCERELY MADE?

God Cannot Be Insincere

When God commanded Moses to go to Pharaoh, and demand that the children of Israel be allowed to go three days journey into the wilderness to hold a feast, God knew before he sent Moses that Pharaoh would refuse (Exodus 3:18–19). Was God sincere? Being a holy and just God, he could not be insincere.

A man may be altogether sincere in giving an invitation that he knows will be refused. A father who knows that his sons will do wrong, still feels constrained to tell them what is right. His warnings and pleadings are sincere; the trouble is in the sons' propensity to disobey.

After the American Civil War, General U. S. Grant offered free pardon to all those in the Confederate army provided they would lay down their arms and go home. He even offered them their horses for use in spring planting. History records that there were little pockets of resistance because of pride and malice. Their refusal to accept it did not change the fact that Grant was sincere in making his offer.

According to Calvinistic theology, the non-elect have all the advantages and opportunities of securing salvation that any other form of theology presents to mankind; Calvinists just maintain that without God's effectual call and new birth lost sinners will not come.

On the other hand, Arminians say that by their free will sinners do come. When Arminians accuse Calvinists of not being sincere in a universal call, the same objections apply to them as far as foreknowledge is concerned. How can the offer of salvation be sincerely offered or made to those whom God foreknows will despise and reject it, especially when their guilt and condemnation will only be increased by their refusal? Arminians admit that God knows beforehand who will accept and who will reject the message, yet they know themselves to be under a divine command to preach to all men, and they do not feel that they act insincerely in doing so.

Election a Secret Decree

I believe the whole answer swings around the fact that election is a secret decree. No preacher has received a revelation from God as to who are and who are not the elect among his hearers. In order to offer the message of salvation to the elect, a preacher must offer it to everyone. Scripture certainly teaches that it should be offered to everyone. Paul wrote,

If thou shalt confess with thy mouth the Lord Jesus, [or Jesus as Lord] and shalt believe in thine heart that God hath raised him from the dead, thou shalt be saved. For with the heart man believeth unto righteousness; and with the mouth confession is made unto salvation. For the scripture saith, Whosoever

believeth on him shall not be ashamed. For there is no difference between the Jew and the Greek: for the same Lord over all
is rich unto all that call upon him. For whosoever shall call upon
the name of the Lord shall be saved.

(Romans 10:9–13)

Addressed to Certain People

The Bible's invitations in the strict sense are not general; on the
contrary, they are addressed to certain people. Here, for example,
are eight such invitations:

- To the thirsty, Christ says, "Come to the waters."
- To the sin-laden, he says, "Come let us reason together."
- To the heavy-laden, Christ says, "Come unto Me."
- To the inquirer, he says, "Come and see."
- To the hungry, Christ says, "Come and dine."
- To the weary, he says, "Come ye yourselves apart."
- To the dead, he says, "Come forth."
- To all, Christ says, "Whosoever will let him come."

The preaching of the New Testament indicates that every gospel message is calculated to bring men and women face to face
with the truth that demands a decision. However, the decision that
is made is not the result of the preacher studying 50 ways to give
an invitation, but it is the result of the convicting ministry of the
Holy Spirit in connection with faithful Bible preaching. In the book
of Acts, you do not find 15 minute messages followed by a pro-
longed invitation. There we find that the Spirit of God opens men's
hearts enabling them to receive Jesus Christ as their Lord and Saviour, or he doesn't. Here are some examples:

- When they heard the gospel "they were pricked in their
  heart, and said . . . What shall we do?" (Acts 2:37)
- "They were not able to resist the wisdom and the spirit by
  which he [Stephen] spake." (Acts 6:10)

- "They were cut to the heart." (Acts 7:54)
- "When they believed . . . they were baptized." (Acts 8:12)
- "While Peter yet spake these things, the Holy Ghost fell on all them which heard the Word." (Acts 10:44)
- "Jews . . . were filled with envy . . . contradicting and blaspheming." (Acts 13:45)
- "They were glad and glorified the word . . . And as many as were ordained to eternal life believed." (Acts 13:48)

Since in this chapter we have been looking at the free offer of the gospel in sincerity, we'll conclude with a quotation from an address by Charles Haddon Spurgeon to his students in the Pastor's College:

I think it is needful that when a minister gets his text, he should say what the text means honestly and uprightly. Too many preachers get a text and kill it. They wring its neck and stuff it with some empty notions and present it upon the table for an unthinking people to feed upon. That man of God does not preach the whole counsel of God who does not let God's Word speak for itself in its own pure language. O, Word, speak for thyself, and be thou heard alone. Suffer me not, O Lord to pervert or misinterpret thine own heaven sent truth. Simple honesty to the pure Word of God is I think requisite to the man who would not shun to declare the whole counsel of God.

CHAPTER FIVE

WHAT IS SALVATION?

Turn us, O God of our salvation, and cause thine anger toward us to cease . . . Show us thy mercy, O Lord, and grant us thy salvation. Surely his salvation is nigh them that fear him; that glory may dwell in our land.

(Psalm 85:4, 7, 9)

Through Rochester, New York, runs the Genesee River between steep and crooked banks. On one occasion a gentleman, who lived in the city, had just arrived by train. He was anxious to go home and greet his wife and children. As he was hurrying along the street nearest the river bank, with a bright vision of home in his mind, he suddenly saw a crowd of people at the river's edge.

"What's the matter?" he shouted.

"A boy is in the river," they said.

"Why don't you save him?"

Then without waiting for a reply, he threw down his bag, ripped off his coat, kicked off his shoes and dove into the water. He grasped the boy in his arms and struggled with him to shore. He brushed the boy's hair out of his eyes, and wiped the water from his face. "Heaven," he said, "it's my own boy!"

He had plunged into the river to rescue somebody else's boy and discovered that he had saved his own. He had received "good measure, pressed down" for a courageous and human act.

Like a similar brave action in almost any city or village in the country, it was big news. The rescue story appeared in the newspapers, who were glad to print such a rescue story with its twist ending.

Father Saves Boy—Discovers Him to Be His Son

Suppose that same father came home some Sunday morning and walked into his church and took a seat in a rear pew after the service had started. At the close of a good message on salvation by the pastor, a young boy responds to the gospel invitation to receive Christ as his Lord and Saviour.

At the end of the service, the father discovers that it is his son who has been saved. Do you think there would have been even a two-line news item about it on the back page of a newspaper? The average, unsaved, city editor would say, "The rescue story is great news, but the boy's conversion has no real news value for our readers."

This is just another proof that the natural man has no ability to make right value comparisons. Man with his natural or carnal mind is a lot more concerned with physical and temporal rescues than he is with spiritual and eternal salvation. In fact we almost take the word "salvation" for granted.

For example, we usually think of the Salvation Army as a good will, charity to help those with physical needs. But that is not what William Booth, who founded the Salvation Army in 1880, intended it to be. He saw it as an army of believers eager to take the gospel of Jesus Christ to men and women that they might be saved from their sins and have eternal life.

It would do us all good to learn and remember the definition of the word "salvation." Webster's Dictionary says the word salvation means (1) the saving of man from the spiritual consequences of sin, (2) a redeemed soul's deliverance from eternal punishment and entrance into heavenly beatitude, (3) deliverance from sin and eternal damnation through the atonement of Christ, (4) redemption.

That is more biblical theology than you would get from many churches in a year. Salvation is important. That is why we began this chapter with a short passage from the Psalms that includes the word salvation three times to emphasize the importance of God's mercy.

What is salvation? What part does grace play in salvation? Only a few Christians would answer, "Everything." But that is not what most churches in the world are preaching today. Since salvation is being distorted and corrupted in many ways, it will help us to study what salvation is not. Here, for example, are two of the most popular perversions of biblical salvation.

Salvation Is Not Reformation

Modern theology puts great emphasis upon the improvement of man and the world. In spite of the fact that newspapers, radio, and television every day are revealing the utter depravity of the human race, many preachers insist that men and women are inherently good. "Although many things are wrong with society, nations, and culture," they say, "religion can improve conditions by education, and character reformation."

To change people as well as environment, church goers are urged to take Jesus as their example and learn his teachings, especially his Sermon on the Mount, for their program of reformation. If men and women learn to follow in the steps of Jesus and apply his teachings to their lives and relationships, they will work out their own salvation.

Preachers are teaching the fatherhood of God and the brotherhood of man. They say just as God was the Father of Jesus, God is the Father of us all, and we are all brothers and sisters who can be peace-loving creatures.

Modern preachers who believe in liberal theology adopt many unbiblical practices of modern science and believe they are establishing the kingdom of God on earth. Needless to say that those who hold to such a view of salvation believe that salvation does not need God's sovereign grace. Salvation according to many liberal churches is the work of man, not of God.

It is quite superfluous to prove that this human philosophy has nothing in common with the biblical gospel of salvation. God's Word teaches that ruined sinners are saved by God's sovereign grace alone through faith alone in the Lord Jesus Christ alone. Christ lived a perfect, sinless life in order to meet all the preceptive demands of the law, and he died a vicarious death to meet all the penal demands of the law on behalf of his elect people. When he rose triumphantly from the dead, he proved beyond all shade of doubt that he had the power and authority to save sinners from their sins.

Salvation Is Not of Man's Will

Surprisingly, it is not only in liberal circles that one meets with a perverted presentation of the truth of salvation. Thousands of pastors and evangelists seek to preach the gospel of Christ by avoiding the doctrine of sovereign grace. They claim that salvation depends for its realization on the will of man.

According to this popular view, salvation is something like a present that is freely and graciously offered, but which one may either refuse or accept. One evangelist recently said that salvation is "a large bucket that a sinner can come and dip anytime he or she pleases." The sinner is offered salvation, chiefly consisting in escape from hell and entrance into heaven after this life, on condition he will accept Christ. Such men tell sinners that God loves everyone, that his Son died for everyone, and that he made it possible for all to be forgiven and go to heaven.

This sounds like pastors and evangelists are preaching the grace of God, but the grace they preach is not sovereign and efficacious. In fact, they say, in effect, that God is powerless to save a sinner from the dominion of sin and death, unless he gives God permission to do so. This is the same as saying that God is limited in what he can do by the reaction of sinners.

This erroneous evangelistic method says, "If the sinner only receives the salvation that is offered to him; if only he will say, 'I accept Christ as my Saviour' all will be well with him and grace can proceed." They also teach that if a sinner is obstinate and declines the earnest invitation to be saved, grace can do nothing for him. Many preachers do not hesitate to openly and boldly declare that God is powerless to save the sinner, unless the sinner gives his consent. In other words, Christ cannot save a sinner unless he permits Christ to proceed with his work of salvation. Here are three quotes from religious leaders in Bible schools and churches:

"God has done all he can to save sinners," says J. Harold Smith, "now it is up to you."

"Hell," says Noel Smith, "is a ghastly monument to the failure of God to save those who are there."

"No man can ever make his bed in Hell," says Dallas Billington of Akron, Ohio, "until God has tried his best to save him."

These statements must be offensive to God, insulting to Christ, and grievous to the Spirit. What these men are saying is that Jesus is willing to save, but his willingness must suffer shipwreck on the rock of man's contrary and refractory will. A common evangelistic appeal says, "Christ stands knocking at the door of your heart, but the key of the door is on the inside, and the Saviour cannot enter to save you unless you open the door."

This appeal is not only dishonoring to Christ, it is a misinterpretation of Revelation 3:20, which has Christ saying, "Behold I stand at the door, and knock: if any man hear my voice, and open the door, I will come in to him, and will sup with him, and he with me." Christ was not speaking to a sinner but to a church that had declined in its attitude toward Christ. The men of the church were bragging about their material self-sufficiency, and needed to recognize their total dependency on the Lord Jesus Christ. They had to open the doors of their hearts and minds to the truth that Christ is the Head of the church.

Many evangelical preachers all over North America are using this erroneous form of evangelism. We say erroneous because true preaching of the gospel never presents a powerless God, or a Christ impotent to save. If a preacher believes that the exercise of God's grace is dependent on the choice of the sinner's will, it follows that he also believes that the persuasion of human language, his appealing voice pleading and begging, will induce the sinner to make the right decision. Some are so bereft of a knowledge of God's saving grace that they will make a statement like this:

> John was under conviction tonight. If only the pastor had got us
> to sing another verse or another invitation hymn, he would have
> been saved.

Thus is the glorious gospel of God's redemptive grace changed from a God-centered message to a man-centered appeal. Such is a perversion of the gospel. Since the salvation being preached in most evangelical churches today is not the salvation taught in the Word, what then is salvation?

SALVATION IS A WORK
MORE GLORIOUS THAN CREATION

Salvation, to be sure, is deliverance from hell and damnation. "He that believeth on the Son," said John the Baptist, "hath everlasting life: and he that believeth not the Son shall not see life; but the wrath of God abideth on him" (John 3:36). Salvation, however, is much more than the mere escape from sin and punishment, or a check on the bank of heaven that is to be cashed after death. Salvation is a wonder work of almighty God, "who quickeneth the dead, and calleth those things which be not as though they were" (Romans 4:17).

Salvation is a work in which God reveals himself to believers. Here is how Paul explains this:

> That the God of our Lord Jesus Christ, the Father of glory, may
> give unto you the spirit of wisdom and revelation in the knowl-
> edge of him: The eyes of your understanding being enlightened;
> that ye may know what is the hope of his calling, and what the
> riches of the glory of his inheritance in the saints, And what is

the exceeding greatness of his power to us-ward who believe, according to the working of his mighty power, which he wrought in Christ, when he raised him from the dead, and set him at his own right hand in the heavenly places.

(Ephesians 1:17–20)

All that Paul presents here is required to save a sinner. For God to take one (who is dead in sin, filled with enmity against God, cursing the Almighty and raising his rebellious fist in the face of the Lord of heaven and earth, walking in darkness and hating the light) and turn him into a saint is greater than God's creation of the universe out of nothing.

To make a rebellious sinner a righteous and holy child of God, who humbly seeks to do God's will, has a great love for God, and daily sings his praises, is the wonderful work of salvation by grace. It places the redeemed and delivered sinner in living fellowship with the glorious company of the saints who make up the family of God. Such a sinner becomes a holy temple of God to the praise of the glory of his grace in the beloved. All this is included in the mighty work of God called salvation!

SALVATION IS AN EXCLUSIVELY DIVINE WORK

Salvation by grace means that salvation is an exclusively divine work, absolutely free and sovereign, in which man has no part at all, and that does not in any sense depend upon the choice of man's will. "So then it is not of him that willeth nor of him that runneth," said Paul, "but of God that sheweth mercy" (Romans 9:16).

Even as the work of creation is of God alone, which he accomplished without the cooperation of the creature, so the work of salvation is exclusively God's work. Adam had no part in his creation. He became an active living creature exclusively by virtue of the creative power of God. In the same way, God gives the sinner a new spiritual life that, in turn, convicts him of his sin and guilt, and gives him the desire, ability and will to repent of his sins and believe in Christ for salvation. His repentance and faith are not exercised in cooperation with God who saves him, but as a result of redemptive grace that calls and regenerates him by the Spirit of God.

Salvation by grace always implies that grace is first. True, "Whosoever will may come," but the will to come is not before grace operates. Another way to state the same truth is by asking the question, "Who makes the whosoevers willing to come?" Only one answer: GOD. The Bible says that believers were spiritually "born, not of the . . . will of man, but of God" (John 1:13).

Here is the story of a man who learned the truth about salvation by grace. Dr. Alexander Carson was born in Scotland in 1776 and graduated with first honors in his class from the University of Glasgow in 1794 when he was only 18 years of age! Ordained in the Presbyterian ministry, he was commissioned to pastor a church in Tubbermore, a small village of only 2,000 persons in Northern Ireland.

One would not expect to hear much about a village preacher who spent all his life in such a small town. God, however, uses men who are sold out to him and his Word. As a diligent student of the Bible, Carson came to the conclusion that a local church with no outside authority ruling over it was the way the early Christian churches operated.

Later he came to another important decision—that baptism was by immersion and for believers only. These findings of course put him in conflict with Presbyterian synods, belief, and practice. When the authorities of the Presbyterian denomination came to put him out of the church one Sunday morning, he asked them to wait until he had finished his morning message and then he would voluntarily retire.

After he had finished preaching, he stepped down from the pulpit and walked down the center aisle. Suddenly, a deacon of the church picked up the large pulpit Bible, swung it on to his shoulder, and marched down the aisle behind his pastor. "Let all who wish to follow the Bible," he shouted to the congregation, "come this way."

Most of the congregation followed them and gathered in a green field nearby where they organized a Baptist church. The blessing of the Lord continued upon that group of Bible believers until it grew to a congregation of over 500 baptized believers in the small town of Tubbermore, which had a population of little more than 2000.

Alexander Carson wrote a book entitled *Baptism, Its Mode and Its Subjects,* which has become a classic on that ordinance. He was a faithful servant of God and the father of 13 children. He never received more than $250 a year, yet he raised hundreds of dollars for Baptist missions. Here is what he had to say about the subject of salvation:

> If God requires any conditions on the part of sinners it is impossible that salvation is of grace. However inconsiderable and easy such conditions may be, however short of the value of what is gained, still when they are performed, they are works and therefore contrary to grace. When they are performed they give ground to glory. If faith, repentance, sincere obedience are the works of men or the product of man's own efforts then his salvation is the fruit of his own labor. If one perishes, because he does not comply with these terms and another is saved on account of them, then salvation is not of grace, but by human merit. The man may glory in the success of his efforts.

SALVATION IS THE DELIVERANCE FROM DEATH AND DARKNESS TO LIFE AND GLORY

It is good once in a while to think about what we have been saved from. Human nature is prone to water down the difference between what we were before conversion and what we are afterwards. Paul the apostle wrote a brilliant description of what the Christian was delivered from in these words:

> And you hath he quickened, who were dead in trespasses and sins; wherein in time past ye walked according to the course of

this world, according to the prince of the power of the air, the spirit that now worketh in the children of disobedience: Among whom also we all had our conversation in times past in the lusts of our flesh, fulfilling the desires of the flesh and of the mind; and were by nature the children of wrath, even as others.

(Ephesians 2:1–3)

Yes, even those of our young people who have been saved from gross sin had the potential to be just as this passage describes the sinner. I remember the incident many, many years ago when my oldest son, Bob, was in Little League baseball, and a ball had been hit or thrown out of the playing field and rolled down a bank under the bridge of the Kanawha River near the field. My son went down under the bridge to retrieve the ball and came upon a scene that he had never seen or imagined before in his life.

A group of "winos" (men who get drunk on cheap wine) were under the bridge. They were greatly intoxicated; some were lying exposed, and one of them was staggering around in his own vomit. It was a horrible scene for a young boy to see. When he didn't come back up the river bank right away, I hurried down to help him hunt for the ball, and then had to try to explain this scene of sin to a young, innocent-minded boy.

What does it mean that apart from grace we are dead in trespasses and sins? It signifies exactly what it says: By nature we are just as dead unto God, righteousness, and all God-honoring works as a corpse in the grave is dead unto all activity of any kind. By nature all are slaves of sin—willing slaves to be sure, but slaves just the same—loving darkness rather than light. The Bible says that apart from the redemptive grace of God, all are children of wrath from their birth, guilty, and because of Adam's transgression, under the divine curse of damnation. The Bible says the carnal mind is death or complete separation from God. To be physically alive but spiritually dead is a miserable plight indeed.

Salvation is such a wonderful subject that we can never tire of reading or talking or writing about it. Here is what that great nineteenth century Baptist preacher, Charles Spurgeon, had to say about salvation and what the Bible really means when it says, "Salvation is of the Lord" (Jonah 2:9).

Oh, to know the full meaning of the words, "Salvation is of the Lord." The Holy Spirit alone can beat this truth into men's minds. A man will lie broken at the foot of a steep cliff, every bone dislocated by his fall, and yet hope to save himself. Piles of sin will fall upon him and bury him, and still his self-trust will live. Mountains of actual transgressions will overwhelm him and floodwaters of guilt will surround him, but he will entertain thoughts of self deliverance. Though crushed to atoms, every particle of our nature reeks with conceit. Though ground to powder, our very dust is pungent with pride. Only the Holy Spirit can render the sinner totally helpless and make him receive the humbling truth, "Salvation is of the Lord."

If deadness in sin is a sinner's position by natural birth, it would be impossible for an emotional and sentimental plea of a preacher to persuade him to seek salvation in Christ. Before redemptive grace takes hold of the sinner and raises him from spiritual death, he will always refuse to accept God's offer of salvation.

In my library is a book entitled *3,285 Bible Questions and Answers* by Emily Filipi. It would be a helpful book for a counselor to young people or for Sunday school teachers to use in their games for students. The questions have to do with persons, countries, books of the Bible, Christmas, promises, prayer, and many other subjects.

However, it lacks the most important question one could ask and the most important answer one could hear. The question was asked 2,000 years ago by a prison official, who was about to commit suicide because an earthquake had opened the prison doors and broke the prisoners' bonds. The official was the jailor of the prison in the city of Philippi, and two of his prisoners were Paul the apostle and Silas, his fellow missionary.

Falling down in front of the missionaries, the jailor asked that most important question. "What must I do," he said, "to be saved?"

And the missionaries responded with the most important answer. "Believe on the Lord Jesus Christ," they said, "and thou shalt be saved, and thy house" (Acts 16:31).

Though Paul and Silas's answer to the Philippian jailor was given in the first century, it is just as important now as it was then. It is the one correct and certain answer to the sinner who wants to know what he must do to be saved from his sin, because for the sinners seeking salvation, the only answer is faith in the Lord Jesus Christ.

CHAPTER SIX

WHO WAS RESPONSIBLE FOR CHRIST'S DEATH?

Ye men of Israel, hear these words; Jesus of Nazareth, a man approved of God among you by miracles and wonders and signs, which God did by him in the midst of you, as you yourselves also know: Him, being delivered by the determinate counsel and foreknowledge of God, ye have taken, and by wicked hands have crucified and slain: Whom God hath raised up, having loosed the pains of death: because it was not possible that he should be holden of it.

(Acts 2:22–24)

The Jew: Dixie's New Target of Hate." That was the headline of a Sunday newspaper article that appeared a short while ago. The writer went on to describe anti-Semitism that is rising in the South. Of course, that is nothing new in Jewish history. They have been blamed for many things and persecuted in the Spanish inquisition and Nazi Germany under Hitler.

Historical Fact

One of the charges brought against Jews was the historical fact that they put Christ to death and the Bible sets for this charge as a fulfillment of prophecy. When the Roman governor, Pilate, saw that he could prevail nothing against the multitude he took water and washed his hands before the multitude, saying, "I am innocent of the blood of this just person: see ye to it."

"Then answered all the people and said, His blood be on us, and on our children" (Matthew 27:25).

It is a historical fact that the Jewish leaders of Christ's day demanded the death of the only perfect person to ever walk on this earth. They undoubtedly stirred up many people to shout for his crucifixion who perhaps did not realize all the particulars involved, but are the Jews of Christ's day totally responsible for the death of God's Son? Did Pilate, by merely washing his hands in a basin of water, rid himself of all guilt? Was Herod acquitted too? Were the Roman soldiers who pounded the nails through his hands and feet just obeying orders and therefore were not guilty?

Divine Sovereignty and Human Responsibility

The first few chapters of the book of Acts provide an answer to this question: "Who was responsible for the death of the Lord Jesus Christ?"

The Bible teaches that there is a divine side and a human side to the Cross: We are removed by nearly two thousand years from the time of Christ's crucifixion in A.D. 30. The men and women who listened to the apostle Peter preach at Pentecost, however, had either witnessed or heard about his death not more than seven or eight weeks before. Burning in their minds was the picture of that rough, cruel, bloody form of execution. They were familiar with the torture and death by Roman crucifixion.

The passage in Acts quoted above brings out the divine and human parts in the death of Christ. Few other places in God's Word speak so plainly of God's sovereignty and human responsibility. One of the definitions of "responsibility" in the dictionary reads, "Answerable as the primary cause, motive or agent, whether evil or good, creditable or chargeable with the result." It is with this definition in mind that I again ask the question, "Who was responsible for Christ's death?" In this chapter we are going to look at three answers to that question. The first answer may come as a surprise or even a shock to some who profess faith in Christ.

THE DIVINE SIDE OF THE CROSS

Infinitely More than Murder

When Peter referred to the death of the Lord Jesus in his sermon at Pentecost, he did not begin by speaking about the brutality or dastardliness of crucifixion. On the contrary, he began by saying that Christ was "delivered up by the determinate counsel and foreknowledge of God" (Acts 2:23).

That is the aspect of Christ's death to which a sinner clings when he knows himself to be lost and undone. Believing sinners are not saved from their sins by the murder of a mere man. They are saved by the vicarious and sacrificial death of the One who was "delivered up by the determinate counsel and foreknowledge of God." To be sure, men conspired to murder Christ, but his death was infinitely more than murder.

His death took place because God planned for it to take place. He was "delivered up by the determinate counsel and foreknowledge of God." The Greek word translated "determinate" here, means "horizon," and the words "determinate counsel" suggest the plan of God, which was within the boundaries of his purpose.

The death of Christ, said Peter in effect, was not an accident or merely brought about by men. It was the visible working out in human history of God's eternal purpose, power, and plan to redeem a people for himself. It was God's way of meeting all the preceptive and penal demands of his law on behalf of those he chose and gave to Christ before the foundation of the world.

Not the God of the Bible

The doctrine of God's sovereignty and supremacy over all things is the most important doctrine in the Bible, and it is the doctrine that is the least taught by modern evangelists, pastors, and writers.

Many Christian leaders need to go back to the Bible and build their sermons and plan their books with God's sovereignty in mind. In many cases, the god presented to the people of the twenty-first century is not the God that the apostles, Augustine, the Reformers, and the Puritans preached.

The god of many sermons and books appears to be more of an object of pity than the biblical God of awe-inspiring reverence and sovereignty. Some say that God the Father purposed the salvation of all mankind. They also say that God the Son died with the express intention of saving the whole race, and that God the Holy Spirit is now seeking to win the world to Christ.

Common observation and fact, however, show that most of the people in the past died in their sins and most of those in the world reject Christ and are on the broad way to destruction. To say that God planned to save everyone is to say that God failed to accomplish what he planned.

Offensive Evangelistic Appeals

Some modern evangelists and pastors use evangelistic appeals that must be offensive to God. For example, one will say, "God is trying to get your attention, but he cannot save you unless you let him." Another says, "God is trying his best to save all mankind, but the reason so many are lost is that the majority will not let him save them." Speaking to sinners, one evangelist said that regarding their salvation, "God has a vote, Satan has a vote, and you have a vote, but you cast the deciding vote."

Those kinds of appeals are the same as saying that the will of sinful man is more powerful than the will of the omnipotent God. Some blame the Devil for the millions who refuse to repent and believe. But that is saying that the Devil is more powerful than God.

One preacher foolishly said, "God has given some of his sovereignty to the devil so he could rule the world." But the Bible teaches that God is sovereign and in absolute control of all creation—including men, angels, Satan, and demons.

Parts of One Comprehensive Plan

Many of today's sermons cannot be identified with what the Bible says about the death of Jesus Christ. The apostles, for example, proclaimed that the death of their Master was a fulfillment of many Old Testament prophecies, such as Psalm 2 and Isaiah 53. They said that God was working out his redemptive purpose to save his elect by the death of his beloved Son, the Lord Jesus Christ.

Our mighty God has a plan, an eternal purpose. History in all its details, even the most minute, is but the unfolding of the eternal purpose of God. His decrees are not successively formed as emergencies arise, but are parts of one comprehensive plan.

We should never think of God suddenly evolving an action or plan or doing something which he had not thought of before. God knew that when George Washington had more than one horse shot from beneath him in the French and Indian War that he would escape injury and lead American forces against England and become the first President of the United States of America. God knew and planned that Napoleon would be defeated at Waterloo and would not conquer Europe. How we should rejoice that God's eternal plan permitted Adolf Hitler to go only so far and then snuffed out his life in suicide. Luke set forth the purpose of God in the early chapters of Acts. Other writers also spoke of God's control of all things and his purpose. Peter wrote that Christ "verily was foreordained before the foundation of the world, but was manifest in these last times for you" (1 Peter 1:20). Paul wrote, "That in the dispensation of the fulness of times he might gather together in one all things in Christ, both which are in heaven, and which are on earth; even in him: In whom also we have obtained an inheritance, being predestinated according to the purpose of him who works all things after the counsel of his own will" (Ephesians 1:10–11).

Paul also said, "And to make all men see what is the fellowship of the mystery, which from the beginning of the world hath been hid in God, who created all things by Jesus Christ: To the intent that now unto the principalities and powers in heavenly places might be known by the church the manifold wisdom of God. According to the eternal purpose which he purposed in Christ Jesus our Lord: In whom we have boldness and access with confidence by the faith of [or through faith in] him" (Ephesians 3:9–12).

Speaking of God's eternal purpose, theologian Dr. Benjamin B. Warfield said,

> The writers of Scripture saw the Divine plan as broad enough to embrace the whole universe of things, and minute enough to concern itself with the smallest details, and actualizing itself with inevitable certainty in every event that comes to pass. In the infinite wisdom of the Lord of all the earth, each event falls with exact precision into its proper place in the unfolding of his eternal plan; nothing, however small, however strange, occurs without his ordering or without its peculiar fitness for its place in the working out of his purposes; and the end of all shall be the manifesting of his glory, and accumulation of his purpose.

THE HUMAN SIDE OF THE CROSS

The Crime of All History

We have looked at the divine side of the cross but what about the human side of the cross? In his sermon on the day of Pentecost, Peter brought the guilty face to face with their crime of murdering Jesus Christ. They were also identified in this prayer by the apostles:

> For of a truth against thy holy child Jesus, whom thou hast anointed, both Herod, and Pontius Pilate, with the Gentiles, and the people of Israel, were gathered together, For to do whatsoever thy hand and thy counsel determined before to be done.
>
> (Acts 4:27–28)

All of these were involved in the crime of all history—the murder of the Son of God! Jewish leaders, who claimed to be under the law of God, violated that law when they murdered Christ. And Gentiles, without the law of God, seared their consciences with what they had done. On the human side, Christ's death was caused by the most grievous sin of all. The only sinless man who ever lived was delivered up by the determinate counsel and foreknowledge of God, and put to death by the crime of men.

Responsibility, Motive, and Intention

This seeming dichotomy bothers some people. "How is it possible," they ask, "for God to decree that men should murder his Son and hold them responsible and punish them for doing so?" Christ's murder is not the only case in which God held responsible those whose sinful conduct was used by him to accomplish his purposes.

For example, consider the case of Judas Iscariot. The Bible says that God decreed that Judas should betray Christ (Zechariah 11:12). Yet God held Judas responsible for what he did. You see, God's motive for using Judas to betray Christ was not the same as Judas's motive for doing so. Responsibility attaches mainly to the motive and intention of the one committing the act.

Most systems of jurisprudence distinguish between a blow inflicted by accident without evil design and a blow delivered with malice aforethought. Apply this to Judas. What was his design when bargaining with the priests? Though God used him and his act of betrayal, Judas acted out of his own sinful desire for money.

Judas did not know that the Pharisees were out to put Christ to death and thought that Christ could escape any of their evil designs. When he found out that they were going to kill him, he went back to the temple to face them. Throwing the 30 pieces of silver on the temple floor, he said, "I have betrayed the innocent blood."

The sound of those coins hitting the marble floor must have been like a death knell ringing in his brain, because he left the Jewish leaders and went out and hanged himself.

As with Judas, so it was with all those involved in the murder of Christ. The Bible says that his murderers crucified him, not merely by human hands, but "by wicked or lawless hands."

They were wicked hands because what they did was motivated by evil intentions.

Someone might object with this argument: "If God decreed that Judas should betray Christ, and that the Jews and Gentiles should crucify him, they could not do otherwise. Therefore they were not responsible for their intentions."

Again the answer has to do with motive and intention. God had decreed that they should sin as they did, but in the actual performance of those sins, they could be judged guilty because their own motives and intentions for sinning were evil.

The Bible does not teach that God produces the sinful dispositions of men and women. But he does restrain and direct them to accomplish his own purposes. Therefore he neither authors nor approves sin.

God's decrees are not the necessitating cause of the sins of men, but the predetermined and prescribed boundaries and directions of men's sinful acts. In the connection with the betrayal of Christ, God did not decree that Jesus should be betrayed by one of his creatures, and then take up a good man, implant his heart with an evil desire, and thus force him to perform the terrible deed in order to execute his decree.

Not so. Scripture is very careful not to present the betrayal of Christ in that way. God decreed the act and Judas as the one to carry it out. John 6:70 says that when Christ chose Judas for the apostolic band, he was already a devil. Judas then proceeded to follow the bent of his depraved nature, just as the Jews and the Gentiles proceeded to do in the crucifixion of Christ.

A simple illustration has helped me to understand this complex problem. A man picks up an aquarium of goldfish and moves it wherever he desires, yet the fish feel themselves free and natural and move unrestrained within the aquarium.

THE PERSONAL SIDE OF THE CROSS

God charged guilty all those who actually took part in the murder of Jesus Christ. But there is a sense in which all of us were represented at that scene of horror. A beautiful Negro spiritual asks, "Were you there when they crucified my Lord?" Yes, we were there because a study of those who were there in person shows that all manner of men were represented at the crucifixion of Jesus Christ.

As we look around at the crowd, we see Roman soldiers, Jews and Gentiles, rich and poor, religious and non-religious, vile and cruel, men and women, interested and just passersby. We can take our pick and, from a study of our own hearts, we can ascertain which group we would be in.

The Roman Soldiers

They spat upon him, nailed him to the tree, and mocked him. What heinous sins they committed! But we should never forget that by the purpose of God, Jesus died for our sins. If we have received the Lord Jesus as our Lord and Saviour, we can say that he fulfilled this prophecy on our behalf:

> But he was wounded for our transgressions, he was bruised for our iniquities: the chastisement of our peace was upon him: and with his stripes we are healed.
>
> (Isaiah 53:5)

While the soldiers were to be blamed for what they did to the Son of God, they represented a large part of every generation since then. They were ignorant about the place Jesus held in God's plan of redemption. It is quite likely that some of them never gave Christ a thought before the day of the crucifixion.

Think of the many men and women who have lived and are living who practiced deliberate ignorance concerning Christ. Fully occupied with the things of this world, they never give him or his gospel of grace for sinners a fleeting thought.

Some of the soldiers at the cross likely laughed at the idea that Jesus dying on the cross was a royal person. But the title on the cross above his head presented this truth: "This is Jesus the King."

Think of how many people whose attitudes toward Christ are like those of the soldiers. They absolutely refuse to honor or subject themselves to Jesus Christ as their Lord and King. "We will not have this man," they say, "to rule over us."

The soldiers stripped Christ and divided his garments among them, and gambled for possession of his seamless coat. They had no compunction about shamefully treating the Son of God and taking what they could from him without a word of thankfulness.

Are there not people in subsequent generations who, by their attitude and anti-biblical ideas, "crucify to themselves the Son of God afresh and put him to an open shame?" (Hebrews 6:6). And think of how many there are to whom Christ has given everything they possess without hearing a word of thanks from them.

Passersby

Though the passersby did not crucify Christ, they did wag their heads and reviled or railed upon him. "Ah!" they said, "Thou that destroyest the temple and buildest it in three days, save thyself and come down from the cross!" (Mark 15:29).

Many people are like that. They regard the crucified and risen Christ as someone to joke about and to mock while they are passing by in this life. Like the passersby at Calvary, they refuse to believe what Christ has said, and they treat him as someone of no account.

Do you know the origin of crucifixion as a form of execution? It began with men taking animals that they thought despicable, like vermin, and nailing them to a post or fence and watching them squirm in agony until they died. When they crucified a man, it was because they thought him to be despicable to their society, and they reveled in the idea of nailing him to a cross and watching him squirm in agony until he died. Speaking in the voice of the psalmist, Jesus said, "But I am a worm, and no man; a reproach of men, and despised of the people" (Psalm 22:6).

The Religious Class

The religious class at the cross consisted of the chief priests, scribes, elders, and Pharisees. You would expect the religious crowd to be respectful, but they laid aside their "piety" and acted worse than others at the cross. Men who had studied the Old Testament, prayed in public, attended the Temple, and gave offerings and tithes were the hypocrites at the crucifixion.

Looking up at Christ on the cross bleeding out his life to "save his people from their sins," (Matthew 1:21) the chief priests mocking said among themselves with the scribes, "He saved others; himself he cannot save. If he be the King of Israel, let him come down from the cross, and we will believe him. He trusted in God; let him deliver him now, if he will have him: for he said, I am the Son of God" (Matthew 27:42–43).

Today there are no worse enemies of Christianity than some who are classed as religious. Like the chief priests of the Jews, they want to make deals with Christ. "If Christ gives us a sign as to who he is," they say in effect, "let him do so and we will believe him." As if the Bible does not have enough evidence as to the identity of Jesus Christ! Why, there is so much evidence supporting the Christ event that those who refuse to believe in him are without excuse.

Others represented by the religious class at the cross are the liberal ministers who deny the divine inspiration of the Bible, the virgin birth, and the deity of Jesus Christ. They also attempt to repudiate the efficacy of his shed blood for the redemption of sinners. And they laugh at the idea of Christ's bodily resurrection from the dead. If some of you are genuine believers in Christ and are attending liberal churches, the Bible has this advice for you:

> Come out from among them, and be ye separate, saith the Lord, and touch not the unclean thing; and I will receive you, and will be a Father unto you, and ye shall be my sons and daughters, saith the Lord Almighty.
>
> (2 Corinthians 6:17–18)

Others who were represented by the religious class at the murder of Christ are the thousands of unbelieving men and women whose names are on evangelical church rolls. They are not interested in repenting from their sins or in believing in Christ as their Lord and Saviour. They have a religious front with no back to it.

They want the respectability of outward religion, but not the responsibility of following Christ.

The General Crowd: The People

The Bible says this group smote their breasts and returned home (Luke 23:48). They did not pound nails into the hands and feet of Christ, revile him, or wag their heads in mockery. They just looked and did nothing. They suffered from indifference and neglect.

That is all a person has to do to be lost—be deliberately indifferent to the Lord Jesus and neglect to believe his offer of salvation from sins. One can attend church, listen to the gospel, and leave without believing it, and he will die in his sins and never get to heaven.

At the cross, some smote their breasts because they feared the supernatural events that took place: the earthquake and the darkness—such an unusual occurrence in the middle of the day! They failed, however, to recognize the significance of the crucifixion. They smote their breasts in fear, but they did not do so as confessed sinners crying to God for mercy.

The Roman Centurion

It is a bit perplexing to study the three accounts of the Roman officer in charge of the crucifixion. Matthew wrote, "Now when the centurion and they that were with him, watching Jesus, saw the earthquake, and those things that were done, they feared greatly, saying, Truly this was the Son of God" (Matthew 27:54)

In Mark's account, he wrote, "And when the centurion, which stood over against him, saw that he so cried out, and gave up the ghost, he said, Truly this man was the Son of God" (Mark 14:39).

And writing his account, Luke wrote, "Now when the centurion saw what was done, he glorified God, saying, Certainly this was a righteous man" (Luke 23:47).

Two accounts have the centurion say that Christ was the Son of God. The other account says he was a righteous man. It is quite possible that he made both statements. If so, was he making a true confession of faith in Christ? Was he admitting that he and his fellow soldiers had crucified an innocent man? Or was he just voicing an opinion about Christ, based on various things he had heard and seen?

Luke said that the centurion glorified God by what he had said. Yet it is likely that he was a pagan Gentile with no training in the religion of the Bible. The priests, elders, and Pharisees had been trained in the Scriptures, yet they were the ones who instigated the conspiracy that led to the murder of Jesus Christ. Though we cannot understand all that was behind the centurion's statement, we can praise God that he could use a pagan to glorify him!

The Dying Thief

Another reason for praising God is what happened to the thief on the cross adjacent to Jesus. Here is one of the most astounding events to take place that day. As the Son of God was dying, he granted the gifts of repentance and faith to a thief and murderer who at first had reviled him when they were put up on the crosses.

Then suddenly he turned his face toward the Lord and said, "Lord, remember me when thou comest into thy kingdom." One preacher described this statement as one of the greatest expressions of faith ever recorded. So far as he knew, he was dying and so was Jesus. Yet somehow he believed that Jesus truly was the Lord and King who had an invisible, spirit kingdom.

"Verily I say unto you," said Jesus, "Today shalt thou be with me in paradise."

The dying thief was representative of many criminals who have been called and regenerated by the Holy Spirit of God. The Lord convicted them of their sin and guilt, and gave them a new desire, ability, and will to repent from their sins and believe in Christ as their Lord and Saviour.

They Thought They Had Won, But God . . .

Those who had conspired to murder Christ looked up at that cross elated, because they thought they had won. Having been jealous of Christ and his popularity with the people, they gloated over getting rid of him. They likely laughed at the sign on the cross saying Jesus was king, because they were blind to the great truth that it would be written of the risen Christ that

> God also hath highly exalted him, and given him a name which is above every name: that at the name of Jesus every knee should bow, of things in heaven, and things in earth, and things under the earth; And that every tongue should confess that Jesus Christ is Lord, to the glory of God the Father.
>
> (Philippians 2:9–11)

This was the most heinous and outrageous crime ever recorded in the annals of human behavior. Yet God used criminal conduct to bring about the most triumphant accomplishment of all time. Only God had the wisdom and power to turn that worst of all human crimes into a once-for-all sacrifice that sinners who believed in him would be redeemed to the praise of his glorious grace!

The Sovereign God of the universe, who launched the exclusive plan to redeem a people for himself, apparently saw to it that all types of men and women were represented at the cross. Surely this shows us that sinners cannot go to heaven unless they go by way of the cross.

> The way of the cross leads home;
> The way of the cross leads home;
> It is sweet to know
> As I onward go,
> The way of the cross leads home.

CHAPTER SEVEN

IS IT FREE WILL OR FREE GRACE?

Every good gift and every perfect gift is from above, and cometh down from the Father of lights, with whom is no variableness neither shadow of turning. Of his own will begat he us with the word of truth, that we should be a kind of first fruits of his creatures.

(James 1:17–18)

L ooking for what others might have to say about James 1:17–18, I consulted a second-hand commentary on the book of James in my library. It was written by one of today's leading, non-denominational, and popular Bible teachers. In the margin adjacent to the comments on James 1:18, a former owner of the book had placed a large question mark.

I thought of several reasons a reader might do that. Using my imagination, I thought perhaps he meant that the commentary was not clear. Then again, I thought he might have felt that the comments brought questions to his mind. After reading the comments for myself, however, I think he likely thought, as I did, that the author's comments were not correct.

A Long-standing Controversy

James 1:18 is one of the strongest verses in the Bible teaching salvation is of the Lord. In it, James says in effect that man is not saved by exercising his own will; instead it is God who saves sinners by his own will. The Holy Spirit put the adjective "own" before God's will to show there is no cooperation between man's will and God's will in the new birth of a sinner.

In this chapter, we are going to examine a controversy that has been going on for centuries. It has to do with God's plan to redeem a people for himself. In spite of all the teaching on the subject, millions of Christians answer these questions in error: Is a sinner saved by the exercise of his own free will? Or is he saved by free grace alone? Salvation by free grace alone means that nothing outside of God himself determines the direction in which his saving grace flows. God is free to choose whom he will because, contrary to what many evangelists say, his will is not directed by the will of man.

Some of them make statements that show they believe that God is unable to save a sinner unless the sinner exercises his will and gives God permission to save him. "God loves you and wants to save you," said one evangelist, "but he cannot do so unless you let him."

The Bondage of the Will

About 500 years ago Martin Luther recognized the cardinal error of the Roman Catholic Church to be its teaching that man's will was the deciding factor in his salvation. In his treatise *The Bondage of the Will,* addressed to the Roman Catholic scholar Erasmus, Luther described free will as "the hinge on which our discussion turns, the crucial issue between us."

He went on to say that "if we know nothing of these things we shall know nothing of Christianity." Luther's purpose in writing was to establish conclusively from God's Word that fallen man's will was in total bondage to sin, and the work of setting it free was the exclusive work of God from first to last.

J. I. Packer describes *The Bondage of the Will* as "undoubtedly the greatest piece of sustained theological writing that Luther ever did, and it stands for all time as the clearest, indeed, the classical elucidation of what the Reformation conflict was all about." Theologian B. B. Warfield described *The Bondage of the Will* in a true sense as the manifesto of the Reformation. Why? Because in his writing, Luther revealed free will to be the watershed of two different systems of belief and practice.

Luther, a convert out of the Roman Catholic priesthood, proved from Scripture that man is fallen, and that fallen man cannot of himself repent and believe the gospel, even though it is his responsibility to do so.

Modern Evangelism

The vast majority of modern evangelists teach and preach a salvation that depends on the free will of man. The evangelist first attacks sin, sin in the individual, then he preaches about Christ and his work on behalf of the sinner, and then he gives the invitation or altar call in which the logical conclusion should be reached.

The evangelist's presentation goes something like this: Sin has been condemned, conscience instructed, and Christ preached. God's will is to save all who unite their will with his. Sometimes an evangelist will even plead over the music for the sinner to prevail against the Devil's effort to hold him captive.

"The will," urges the evangelist, "is free, free to break with the Devil, free to lay hold upon the hope set before it, free to let God come into the heart, free to believe and accept or disbelieve and reject the overtures of redemptive grace. God has done all he can do; eternity hangs on the decision of the human will." Evangelists speak as though God had limited himself forever when he gave man a free will. Is this what the Bible teaches?

FREE WILL'S FALSE STARTING POINT

Inadequate Conception of the Fall

When Adam sinned, he died spiritually. Communion with God ceased. Adam's heart was now estranged from God, and his whole nature became hostile to the character and laws of his Maker. The entire human race has inherited the Adamic nature. Men's minds and hearts are at enmity with God.

The Bible says, "For they that are after the flesh do mind the things of the flesh; but they that are after the Spirit the things of the Spirit . . . . Because the carnal mind is enmity against God: for it is not subject to the law of God, neither indeed can be" (Romans 8:5, 7).

A "free willer," or person who believes in free will has an inadequate conception of man's fall into sin. In Scripture the heart denotes man's affection. The affection is the seat of all desires and motivates the will. "I want" always comes before "I will."

Free Will Only in the Physical Realm

Man is free to do anything he desires and is able to do. Being dead in sin, however, he only desires the things of this world and cannot set his affection on God and his spiritual kingdom. In fact, the Bible says there is not one person who understands the things of God or seeks after him unless God causes him to be born again.

Since the heart or affection motivates the will, the will is in bondage to the things of this world and totally unable to have a right relationship with the spiritual world of God. So we can say that the will of man is free, but only in the physical realm. To become right with God, the Lord must make one free. "If the Son, therefore, shall make you free," said Jesus, "ye shall be free indeed" (John 8:36).

Total Depravity and Total Inability

Only God can so change a man that he has a new desire, ability, and will to repent of sins and believe in Christ for the freedom offered in his gospel. He would never come on his own for freedom in Christ because all men are totally depraved. This does not mean that every man is guilty of all kinds of sin. But it does mean that every faculty of man—his curiosity, his ego, his reason, his affection, his conscience, his memory, and his will—has been touched and distorted by sin. The inability under which every man labors is not an inability to exercise his will, but an inability to will holy thoughts, actions and words that please God. A man who has never been born again may perform actions which are good in themselves such as love his children, work to please his employer, and be courteous toward others.

A person can be socially acceptable, but being a sinner, his motives are carnal and he cannot please God. In addition the Bible says he is "dead in trespasses and sins," or dead spiritually (Ephesians 2:1, 5). With such a strong statement in Scripture, one is in error who says that a spiritually-dead man can contribute toward his own spiritual resurrection.

Some argue, "If that is true, man is nothing but a log, a piece of cement, a robot."

Not so. Man is a creature of God, made in the image of God (Genesis 1:26), but after the fall of Adam and Eve in the garden, all their descendants possess fallen wills, and therein lies the confusion. Man can do nothing to effect his new birth because it is the exclusive, sovereign, and independent work of the Holy Spirit. "Salvation," said Jonah, "is of the Lord."

FREE WILL'S CONFUSION

Free Agency and Human Responsibility

Those who hold to the doctrines of sovereign grace and refuse to believe that man is saved by his free will are often accused of not believing in human responsibility. Nearly all those who teach that sinners are saved because they exercise their free will, confuse free will with free agency or human responsibility. Man's responsibility is in no way lessened or softened by his plunge into sin. Free will and human responsibility are fundamentally different and must not be confused with each other. This distinction is vital. A theology that fails to make this distinction is a defective theology.

The notion that man is responsible only for what he has ability to perform is a delusion. It is as foolish as the drunkard who pleads innocence for criminal offenses committed on the ground of his craving for liquor. Such a plea is to measure responsibility by ability in the matter of sin against the absolute law of God.

In other words the more sinful I become, the less responsible I become. Such distorted reasoning is making headway with humanists and some psychologists, but has no place with the God of Scripture. We are accountable to him in every respect, in every thought, word, and deed. Our responsibility is to render perfect obedience and satisfaction to the moral law of the Ten Commandments.

Lust and Self-Enticement

That we are unable to render this perfect obedience is obvious. Nevertheless it is required. By transgression Adam, our first father, forfeited this ability, and men—being born in sin—now grovel in the miry pit of their lusts and rebellions. They are prisoners of their own sinful natures. The Bible says that "every man is tempted, when he is drawn away of his own lust, and enticed. Then when lust hath conceived, it bringeth forth sin: and sin, when it is finished, bringeth forth death" (James 1:14–15).

Men do not desire God, and they detest the idea of deliverance. Paul said, "There is none that understandeth, there is none that seeketh after God" (Romans 3:11). Like the mad demoniac of Gadara, man by nature says to Christ, "What have I to do with thee?" (Mark 5:7). Man's will is ruled over by the iron rod of the lusts of his own heart. "For out of the heart," said Jesus, "proceed evil thoughts, murders, adulteries, fornications, thefts, false witness, blasphemies. These are the things which defile a man" (Matthew 15:19).

Man's Inner, Personal Ethic

This does not mean that a man is not fully responsible and accountable to God. Even though a sinner's conscience is marred and defiled, it bears perpetual witness to personal responsibility, "which show the works of the law written in their hearts, their conscience also bearing witness, and their thoughts the mean while accusing or else excusing one another; in the day when God shall judge the secrets of men by Jesus Christ according to my gospel" (Romans 2:15–16).

This is to say that every sinner has a personal ethic that he does not obey. He knows in his mind and heart that he does not live up to the moral level of his own internal ethic. As theologian William G. T. Shedd said, "Every man, whatever be the grade of his intelligence, knows more than he puts in practice" (*Sermons to the Natural Man*, p. 84).

Paul described the failure of humans to practice what they know, when he wrote that men have no excuse "because that, when they knew God, they glorified him not as God, neither were thankful: but became vain in their imagination, and their foolish heart was darkened. Professing themselves to be wise, they became fools" (Romans 1:20–23). Therefore, it is not only dangerous for a man not to obey his own inner, personal ethic, but it is the attitude of a dark, foolish heart. There is no more illogical position than that of the atheist who says there is no God, and the Bible rightly calls him a fool.

The Baptist Confession of Faith

Since there is such confusion between free will and fallen will, let us take the time to read what The Philadelphia Confession of Faith has to say. A few years ago, it was the prominent confession of Southern Baptist Churches. Chapter Nine has this to say about free will:

1. God has indued the will of man with that natural liberty and power of acting upon choice, that it is neither forced, nor by any necessity of nature determined to do good or evil.
2. Man, in his state of innocency, had freedom and power to will and to do that which was good and well-pleasing to God, but yet, was mutable, so that he might fall from it.
3. Man, by his fall into a state of sin, hath wholly lost all ability of will to any spiritual good accompanying salvation; so as a natural man, being altogether averse from that good, and dead in sin, is not able by his own strength to convert himself, or to prepare himself thereunto.
4. When God converts a sinner, and translates him into the state of grace, he freeth him from his natural bondage under sin and by his grace alone enables him freely to will and to do that which is spiritually good; yet so as that by reason of his remaining corruptions, he doth not perfectly, nor only will, that which is good, but doth also will that which is evil.
5. The will of man is made perfectly and immutably free to good alone in the state of glory only.

FREE WILL'S DANGEROUS RESULTS

Preachers of a Free-will Gospel Are Without Excuse

The error of free will distorts the biblical doctrine of the new birth. Many evangelicals believe they are strong at this point, when in fact they have so twisted the doctrine of the new birth that it no longer means what the Bible says it means. Though James 1:18 definitely says that believers were begotten by God's own will, modern evangelists ignore, twist, or pervert this plain statement by preaching that men must exercise their own natural will to be born again.

God knew how sinful man can disobey, distort, and disbelieve even such a clear statement as James 1:18. Therefore he moved John to explain the new birth in such a way that those who preach a free-will gospel are without excuse for confusing faith, repentance, and regeneration.

"But as many as received him," he wrote, "to them gave he power to become the sons of God, even to them that believe on his name" (John 1:12).

Many evangelists quote this verse, but they rarely if ever quote what John said next, when he explained how the new birth is accomplished. He said that believers "were born, not of blood, nor of the will of the flesh, nor of the will of man, but of God" (John 1:13).

Could any words be more explicit? The infallible Word of God says that a sinner is born again not by blood or family connections, not by the energy of the flesh, and not by the will of man, but by God alone. Millions of Christians are confused or in error about the new birth because they have been taught that faith and repentance come before and effect the new birth.

It's almost as though men preach that God must come as a suppliant to obtain permission before he can perform the work of regeneration. The idea in most evangelical circles is that God is obliged to do this miracle for every man who fulfills the requirements. But God is not like an automatic coin machine that responds when the coin drops into the slot.

New Birth Comes First

Faith and repentance come as the result of the new birth, which is an exclusive, independent, and sovereign work of the Holy Spirit. One could not repent and believe in Christ if he were not first born again. Faith and repentance are spiritual functions, which rise up in the spirit when the great Physician has completed the removal of the sinful heart of stone, and ingrafted a new heart that is sensitive to the Lord's demands for repentance and faith.

Repentance and faith, then, are not natural to men, but are gifts of God that come after the new birth and after one is convicted of his sin and guilt. The new birth is a supernatural work impossible for man to effect. And without the new birth, it is spiritually impossible for a person to repent and believe in Christ. By the same token, it is spiritually impossible for a person not to believe after he has been born again.

The New Birth Is Not a Four-step Formula

When Christ informed Nicodemus that he must be born again, he stripped him of all self-reliance, and brought him once and for all to an end of himself. The Lord affirmed that Nicodemus lay entirely at the disposal of the Holy Spirit who blows, like the wind, where he wills. He did not at the same time console Nicodemus by giving him a "do-it-yourself kit" so that Nicodemus could bring about his own spiritual birth. To oversimplify the gospel into a formula, by which man is urged to manipulate his own spiritual birth, encourages deception.

That formula says, "First, acknowledge your sin; second, believe in Christ; third, ask him into your heart; fourth, thank him for saving you." Then the preacher tells the person he has been born again.

Scripture teaches that repentance and faith must be urged on all men, and the sinner must be urged to call on the name of the Lord. But this is quite different from the use of a four-step formula when there is no new birth and no conviction of sin. If this little four-step formula is all a sinner has to do, why didn't the apostles use it? Why wade through a book such as Romans, Galatians, or Ephesians?

The Analogy of Birth

I'm reminded of the story of a little boy watching a butterfly trying to get out of a cocoon. Watching the butterfly struggle with the little threads that bound the wings to the chrysalis, the boy said, "Wow, that wasn't easy."

We must remember the analogy of birth when speaking of regeneration. The Lord Jesus Christ said to Nicodemus, "Ye must be born again." That was not a command, but the statement of a self-evident truth. Is there a living creature in the whole world who has decided the time or details of his birth? Likewise there is not one sinner dead in sin who has willed himself, or conveyed himself by an act of decision, into the new birth.

Why then preach the new birth? By this doctrine we learn the awful plight of man, and the same time our attention is directed to the almighty power of God. Man must be convicted of his impotence to save himself.

Nowhere in the Bible does God command his servants to preach that men merely make a decision. A decision is only a fragment, a part of man's duty toward God. The Greek word translated in our English Bible as "repentance" is *metanoia*. And, according to *Strong's Greek Dictionary*, means, "compunction (for guilt including reformation); by implication reversal of (another's) decision." If you look up "repent" in the *Merriam Webster's Collegiate Dictionary*, you will find this definition: "1. to turn from sin and dedicate oneself to the amendment of one's life. 2. a: to feel regret or contrition. b: to change one's mind." Christian repentance, then, is a sincere, wholehearted turnabout.

The Debt We Owe to Tyndale

Anyone who can read and speak English owes a debt to William Tyndale. He was one of the early reformers who laid down his life for the cause of truth. Tyndale wanted the English-speaking world to have the New Testament in their native language instead of Latin or Greek, which the common man did not speak or understand.

The Roman Catholic Church vehemently opposed him and hounded him out of England, chased him from town and countries in Europe, and finally captured him and put him to death.

Before his death, however, he had translated the Greek New Testament into English and smuggled hundreds of copies into his native land. Listen to the words of this brilliant, brave, arduous Christian as he, like Luther, goes right to the core of the subject of free will and the Roman Catholic Church. He said,

Why doth God open one man's eyes and not another's? Paul in Romans 9:19, 20 forbiddeth to ask why; for it is too deep for man's capacity. God we see is honoured thereby, and his mercy set out and the more seen in the vessels of mercy. But Romanists can suffer God to have no secret, hid to himself. They have searched to come to the bottom of his bottomless wisdom: and because they cannot attain to that secret, and being too proud to leave it alone, and to grant themselves ignorant, with the apostle, that knew no other than God's glory in the elect; they go and set up free will with the heathen philosophers, and say that a man's free will is the cause why God chooseth one and not another, contrary unto all the scripture. (*An Answer to Sir Thomas More's Dialogue*, Parker Society reprint, 1850, p. 191)

CHAPTER EIGHT

Does Prophecy Have Pivotal Passages?

For the prophecy came not in old time by the will of man: but holy men of God spake as they were moved by the Holy Ghost.

(2 Peter 1:21)

Shortly after I was converted to Christ in the spring of 1942, I was given a *Scofield Reference Bible* by a pastor in my home town of New Castle, Pennsylvania. As I read it, I accepted Scofield's footnotes as though they were as accurate as the Bible. This made me an ardent believer in the pretribulational, dispensational, premillennial second coming of Jesus Christ.

Over 61 years of Bible study, however, I was compelled by the truth to reject Scofield's dispensational and premillennial interpretation of the prophetic passages in the Bible. I was like the Jews about whom Paul the apostle said, "For I bear them record that they have a zeal for God, but not according to knowledge" (Romans 10:2).

No Change, No Growth

Some think it is a mark of weakness for a preacher or any Christian to change his mind. But when we think about it, it would be foolish for one to maintain what he learned in his youth for the rest of his life. Christians need to change their minds on a regular basis if they ever expect to enjoy spiritual growth.

The famous literary figure James Russell Lowell said, "There are only two classes of men that never change their mind, fools and dead men." And Charles H. Spurgeon said, "To confess you were wrong yesterday is only to acknowledge that you are a little wiser today; and instead of being a reflection on yourself it is an honor to your judgment, and shows you are improving in the knowledge of the truth."

Examples of Scofield's Many Errors

The notes in the *Scofield Reference Bible* are interesting and, unless one has been prepared beforehand, he will find it difficult to detect the many errors they contain. I won't go into all the details about why I now reject Scofield's notes, but I want to give you one or two examples of how erroneous Scofield was.

John the apostle wrote, "For the law was given by Moses, but grace and truth came by Jesus Christ" (John 1:17). Here is what Scofield said about that verse as recorded in the 1945 edition: "The point of testing is no longer legal obedience as the condition of salvation, but acceptance or rejection of Jesus Christ with good works as a fruit of salvation."

Writing in his first epistle (3:7), John said, "Little children, let no man deceive you: he that doeth righteousness is righteous, even as he is righteous." Commenting on this verse, Scofield wrote, "Righteousness here, and in the passages having marginal references to this, means the righteous life which is the result of salvation through Christ. The righteous man under law became righteous by doing righteously; under grace he does righteously because he has been made righteous."

Both of these comments are contrary to God's plan to save a people for himself. In his comments, Scofield actually taught the error that there are two ways to be saved—one by obedience to the law and the other by grace through faith in Christ. Publishers saw these notes to be so unscriptural that they deleted them from the modern edition. But that did not change the fact that Scofield believed what he had written.

Scofield was not even right on his definition of dispensations. If Scofield was wrong on salvation and dispensations, think how wrong he must have been on his ideas about prophecy and eschatology!

A Whole New Perspective

I found there are three pivotal passages that helped me to reject the errors of Scofield and of all those writers who followed in his train. A "pivot" is "a person or thing on which something turns or depends."[5] In the light of that definition, it is obvious that the prophetic scriptures contain some pivotal passages. In this chapter we are going to look at Matthew 21:43, Daniel 9:26–27, and Romans 11:26. I found the study of these pivotal passages gave me a new perspective of the subject of prophecy—a perspective I did not enjoy when I was a young Christian.

THE TRANSFER OF THE KINGDOM OF GOD

Christ's Word of Condemnation

The first pivotal passage we are going to look at is Matthew 21:43, which is part of the parable about the vineyard that Christ told in the temple. In that parable, he told about a vineyard owner who let his vineyard out to tenant farmers. When he sent his servants to receive the fruit of the vineyard, the tenant farmers beat one, stoned one, killed one, and stoned another. The land owner sent more servants, but the tenant farmers treated them in the same way.

Then he decided to send his son saying, "They will reverence my son." But when the tenant farmers saw the son, they conspired together saying, "This is the heir; come let us kill him, and let us

---

[5]Webster's New World Pocket Dictionary.

seize on his inheritance." So they grabbed the son and dragged him out of the vineyard and slew him.

After he told this parable, Jesus addressed this question to the Jewish leaders: "When the Lord therefore of the vineyard cometh, what will he do unto those husbandmen?"

The Jewish leaders said that the landowner should destroy the tenant farmers and let out his vineyard unto other tenant farmers who would "render him the fruits in their seasons."

Little did the Jewish leaders know that Jesus had used the parable as a means of confronting them and to expose their wickedness. Then, speaking of himself as the stone, he reminded them of the Scriptures that said, "The stone which the builders rejected, the same is become the head of the corner: this is the Lord's doing, and it is marvelous in our eyes." Then he spoke the words of the prophetic pivotal passage—the subject of this chapter.

"Therefore I say unto you," said Jesus, "The kingdom of God shall be taken from you, and given to a nation bringing forth the fruits thereof. And whosoever shall fall on this stone shall be broken: but on whomsoever it shall fall, it will grind him to pieces" (Matthew 21:43–44).

When the Jewish leaders heard these words of condemnation, they knew that Jesus was talking about them. It is likely they had read in Isaiah 5 about how God had called Judah a vineyard and had said he would lay it waste because its people had become unjust and unrighteous. The Bible says that when the Jewish leaders had heard the parable from Christ, "they perceived that he spake of them. But when they sought to lay hands on him, they feared the multitude, because they took him for a prophet" (Matthew 21:45–46).

Nation Means More than Race

Scofield said "a nation" meant the Gentiles in general. But Christ didn't say "Gentiles," he said, "nation." This is the first time the word nation appears in the New Testament. The Lord Jesus went through his 3 years of ministry before he ever uttered the word "nation." And the first time he used it, he said the kingdom of God would be taken from the Jews and "given to a nation bringing forth the fruits thereof."

The Greek word translated "nation" is *ethnos* which, according to *Strong's Greek Dictionary*, means "a race, a tribe, a foreign (non-Jewish) one (usually by impl. pagan): Gentile, heathen, nation, people." Christ was saying that the kingdom with all its privileges would be taken from the Jewish nation and given to a new race or tribe or people that was not ethnic Israel.

There are 11 Hebrew words that have been translated "nation" in the Old Testament of the English Bible, but the one used the most predominantly is *goy* from the same root as the word *gevah*, a word that means "a person or body." Is there some significance in this definition and the fact that the church is called the "body" of Christ? Paul wrote, "That the Gentiles should be fellow heirs, and of the same body, and partakers of his promise in Christ by the gospel" (Ephesians 3:6).

The Death Knell of Judaism

Jesus was saying that the Jewish nation was being replaced by the one nation, the church or body of Jesus Christ. Here is the beginning of the "mystery" that Paul wrote about in his epistles. This parable of the vineyard that Christ relates in Matthew 21:33–46 was fulfilled in history. Unwittingly, the Jewish leaders had predicted their own destruction when they said the Lord of the vineyard should destroy the unfaithful and rebellious tenant farmers, and replace them with men who would be faithful in their service to him (Matthew 21:41). That prediction came true when the Roman armies destroyed the city of Jerusalem and its temple in A.D. 70.

By "a nation," then, Jesus meant the church and that the kingdom of God and all its privileges would be taken from the unfaithful and rebellious Jewish nation and given to the people who made up his church. What he said was the death knell of the Jewish nation and Judaism, its apostate religion.

Scofield's Two Kingdoms

Scofield missed the meaning of Christ's parable, because he said there is a dispensational difference between the kingdom of heaven and the kingdom of God (*Scofield Reference Bible*, p. 1029). I foolishly believed that explanation for years.

Then, one day I took the time to study every passage in the Gospels that contained a reference to the kingdom of God or the kingdom of heaven. When I did, it was obvious that Scofield was wrong, because Christ used the kingdom of God and the kingdom of heaven interchangeably. To him there was only one kingdom.

The Church Is Spiritual Israel

This nation, the church, is spiritual Israel, the believers in every nation who "bring forth fruit unto God." It took awhile for the Jews like Peter, Paul, and the rest of the apostles to get this straight, but when they did they preached it so zealously that the Jews became furious and persecuted them for preaching in essence that the church of Christ had replaced the apostate religion of Judaism.

In his first epistle, chapter two, Peter, whose name means rock, said that Jesus Christ was a living stone and chosen by God to be the chief cornerstone of the Church. In doing so, he was quoting the psalmist who said, "The stone which the builders refused is become the head stone of the corner" (Psalm 118:22).

Some Facts about That Holy Nation

He also said that believers were "a chosen generation, a royal priesthood, a holy nation, a peculiar people." His Christian readers, he said, were not that nation or people of the past, but had become God's special people or nation that had obtained mercy. The universal church of Christ (made up of all genuine believers) alone is the holy nation through which God is accomplishing his eternal purpose. Here are some facts about the people of that holy nation:

1. God has not chosen any other, but "he hath chosen us in him before the foundation of the world" (Ephesians 1:4).
2. He has not adopted any other but he has "predestinated us unto the adoption of children by Jesus Christ to himself" (Ephesians 1:5).
3. God has not accepted any other but "hath made us accepted in the beloved" (Ephesians 1:6).
4. The inheritance is not promised to any other but "according to the riches of his grace wherein he hath abounded towards us in all wisdom and prudence" (Ephesians 1:7, 8).
5. He has not revealed his will to any other but he has "made known unto us the mystery of his will" (Ephesians 1:9).
6. God's will is not to accomplish his redemptive purpose through two different bodies of people, the church and ethnic Israel, but only through the church. In Ephesians 1:10 Paul wrote, "that in the dispensation of the fulness of times he might gather together in one all things in Christ, both which are in heaven, and which are on earth; even in him."

National Desolation

Hal Lindsey and other dispensational futurists are leading people astray when they keep putting emphasis on the prophecies being fulfilled by God dealing with ethnic Israel in the future. Their error is exposed when we learn, not only what Christ predicted in this pivotal passage of Matthew 21:43–44, but what he did not say.

For example, Christ did not say that Old Testament Israel would some day get the kingdom back that was taken away from them. What Jesus said was final. The kingdom of God with all of its privileges would be taken away from the Jewish nation and given to the church. This finality of Judah as a nation is underlined by Paul in 1 Thessalonians 2:14–16:

For ye, brethren, became followers of the churches of God which in Judaea are in Christ Jesus: for ye also have suffered like things of your own countrymen, even as they have of the Jews: Who both killed the Lord Jesus, and their own prophets, and have persecuted us; and they please not God, and are contrary to all men: Forbidding us to speak to the Gentiles that they might be saved, to fill up their sins always: for the wrath is come upon them to the uttermost.

For the wrath of God to come upon a nation to the uttermost must mean the utter destruction of that people as a nation. When Jesus looked over Jerusalem and declared the Jews' unwillingness to receive him as their Messiah, he said, "Behold your house is left unto you desolate." Was he speaking of the house of Israel or the temple? In either case, it was a prophecy of the end of the Jewish nation and its apostate religion.

For more than 1,800 years, the Bible-believing leaders of the church believed and taught that the church was the fulfillment of Christ's parable of the vineyard. It wasn't until Irving and Darby introduced their dispensational futurism that Christian people in many churches and Bible colleges embraced their wrong interpretation of biblical prophecy. Their errors were spread even further with the appearance of The *Scofield Reference Bible*. They were led to believe that Israel would come back as a nation after the church age failed. But nothing in the Bible even hints at such an idea.

DANIEL'S 70 WEEKS OF YEARS
(DANIEL 9:24–27)

The Wrong Use of a Word

Do you think that a whole school of prophecy could base its interpretation upon the wrong use of a word? Do you think that one of the greatest fulfillments of prophecy concerning our Lord Jesus Christ could be so twisted that it is applied to the Antichrist instead of our Saviour? Well, it has happened and that is why Daniel 9:26–27 is another great pivotal passage of Scripture.

In his prophecy (9:24–27) Daniel wrote that 12 different things were going to happen in 70 weeks by which is meant 70 weeks of years or 490 years. Looking back from the year 2003, we can say those 12 events were not predicted to be fulfilled some 2,400 years or more into the future, but in 490 years. Therefore they have already been fulfilled. Here is what Daniel wrote in verses 25–26:

> Know therefore and understand, that from the going forth of the commandment to restore and to build Jerusalem unto the Messiah the Prince shall be seven weeks, and threescore and two weeks: the street shall be built again, and the wall, even in troublous times. And after threescore and two weeks shall Messiah be cut off, but not for himself: and the people of the prince that shall come shall destroy the city and the sanctuary; and the end thereof shall be with a flood, and unto the end of the war desolations are determined.

Now read those two verses again with the modifying clauses removed:

> From the . . . commandment to . . . build Jerusalem unto the Messiah, the Prince, shall be seven weeks, and three-score and two [a total of 69] weeks: . . . And after [not "in," but "after"] threescore and two [or 69] weeks [or 483 years] shall Messiah be cut off, but not for himself: and the people of the prince that shall come shall destroy the city and the sanctuary . . .

Webster's Dictionary defines "after" as meaning, "subsequently in time or place; later in time; subsequent to; later than" and the word "in" as "indicating inclusion within space, time or physical surroundings."

By no stretch of the imagination could "after" ever be twisted to mean "in." Yet all who believe that the 70th week or seven years of Daniel's prophecy is still future, base their entire interpretation on the fallacy that "after" can mean "in."

The False Time Gap Theory

The simple conclusion is this: Since the Messiah was to be cut off "after" the 69th week, he must have been cut off in the 70th week. Therefore the prophecy said as clearly as words can express an idea that the Messiah was to be cut off in the 70th week. Since the prophecy was fulfilled when Christ was crucified, then the crucifixion took place in the 70th week and not in the 69th week as dispensational futurists claim.

By teaching that Christ died during the seven years of the prophetic 69th week, is to deny the truth that he was crucified during the seven years of the prophetic seventieth week. Dispensational futurists also say there is a giant time gap between the 69th and 70th week, and the events predicted for the 70th week of seven years remain yet to be fulfilled some 1,973 years later!

Therefore the time gap theory is false teaching that denies the Word of God. The only logical or scriptural conclusion for a believer is that Christ died "after" the 69th week and "in" the 70th week of Daniel's prophecy.

The Verb "Confirm" and the Pronoun "He"

The second great error that futurists make concerning the 70th week of Daniel is a misinterpretation of the word "confirm." Read slowly these first six words of Daniel 9:27: "And he shall confirm the covenant." The word "confirm" means "to give certainty, to ratify," but it *never* means "to make."

Therefore to "confirm" a covenant does not and cannot mean the making of a new covenant, but simply the ratification of an existing covenant. Notice also the pronoun "he." This pronoun of necessity, must refer to an antecedent noun. Eliminating the modifying clauses, the previous sentence reads this way: "Messiah shall be cut off and the people of the prince that shall come shall destroy the city and he shall confirm the covenant."

The pronoun "he" has to refer either to "Messiah" or to "the Prince that shall come." All pretribulationists and dispensational futurists say that "the Prince that shall come" is the Antichrist. It is more biblical, however, to say that the pronoun "he" refers to the Messiah, for this simple reason.

English grammar demands it.

A pronoun cannot have as its antecedent the object of a modifying clause. Note the subject of the sentence: "The people of the prince that shall come shall destroy the city and the sanctuary." The "he" of verse 27 cannot properly refer to the people, neither can it refer to the object of the modifying clause, "of the prince."

The pronoun "he" can only correctly refer to the Messiah of verse 26. The sentence therefore could be read to mean, "And he [the Messiah] shall confirm the covenant." This is true as well because the Messiah is the only person who had a covenant that could have been confirmed. Let's look at the proofs of how this great pivotal passage of Daniel was fulfilled.

1. Jerusalem was restored under Ezra and Nehemiah.
2. They built the streets and walls in troublous times, as Nehemiah so graphically describes in his book.
3. Jesus was cut off at the time predicted. "And they crucified him" (Matthew 27:35).
4. It was the cutting off or crucifixion of Jesus Christ that finished the transgression. Just before he was crucified, Jesus said to the Jewish leaders, "Fill ye up then the measure of your fathers . . . That upon you may come all the righteous blood shed upon the earth, from the blood of righteous Abel unto the blood of Zacharias, whom ye slew between the temple and the altar" (Matthew 23:32, 35).
5. In giving his life on the cross, Jesus Christ made an end of sins. "For then must he often have suffered since the foundation of the world: but now once in the end of the world hath he appeared to put away sin by the sacrifice of himself" (Hebrews 9:26).
6. In being crucified, he, Christ made reconciliation for iniquity. "God was in Christ, reconciling the world unto himself, not imputing their trespasses unto them; and hath committed unto us the word of reconciliation" (2 Corinthians 5:19).

7. Christ's death and resurrection brought in everlasting righteousness. "For he hath made him to be sin for us, who knew no sin; that we might be made the righteousness of God in him" (2 Corinthians 5:21).
8. Jesus Christ's coming sealed up the vision and prophecy. "But those things, which God before had shewed by the mouth of all his prophets, that Christ should suffer, he hath so fulfilled" (Acts 3:18).
9. Christ was anointed at his baptism and shortly thereafter he said he had been anointed. "The Spirit of the Lord is upon me, because he hath anointed me to preach the gospel to the poor" (Luke 4:18).
10. The Lord Jesus did confirm the Covenant. In fact Christ is called "The messenger of the Covenant" in whom God delights (Malachi 3:1). What Covenant? The Mosaic covenant with Israel. The Lord extended and honored it during his public ministry (Matthew 15:24). Grace was being lavished during his ministry where the law had failed. Christ gave forth the precious love, grace, and mercy on Jews and Gentiles alike.
11. Jesus Christ's death and resurrection caused the sacrifice and oblation to cease. "Every priest standeth daily ministering and offering oftentimes the same sacrifices, which can never take away sins: But this man, after he had offered one sacrifice for sins forever, sat down on the right hand of God" (Hebrews 10:11–12).
12. Lastly, instead of the city being destroyed within the remainder of the 70th week, the prophecy spoke of "the prince that *shall come shall destroy the city*" (Daniel 9:26, emphasis added). The verbs "shall come" and "shall destroy" pointed to future events to take place after the Christ event.

Forty Days and Forty Years

Because he is merciful, God did for Jerusalem what he did for Nineveh under Jonah's preaching. God's decree against Nineveh was destruction within 40 days. In other words, God gave them 40 days to repent. They did repent, and the city was saved.

Though John the Baptist told the Jews of Jesus Christ, and Christ himself preached and did many wonderful works in their midst, the Jews rejected and crucified him. God gave the Jewish nation 40 years to repent of their wickedness, which included their murder of Christ and their vicious persecution of his saints. When they failed to repent, the Lord used the Roman armies under Titus to make the city of Jerusalem desolate, and the nation's place with God was given to the church.

All the prophecies concerning the 70 weeks, all 12 of them, were fulfilled. Let me again emphasize that the prophesy of Daniel's 70 weeks is a prophesy concerning our Lord Jesus Christ and not a prophesy concerning some future Antichrist. If modern speculators in prophecy would just check the history of Christianity, they would discover that this was the prevalent belief among Christians up to 1830—the time when dispensational and premillennial futurism was introduced to local churches and Bible colleges all over North America.

AND SO ALL ISRAEL SHALL BE SAVED
(ROMANS 11:26)

The Exclusive Way of Salvation

Over many years, a controversial and disputed subject among Christians is the subject of Israel in Romans 9–11. It seems to be a very difficult thing for some to interpret what Paul meant by Israel. Here are the most controversial verses in those three chapters:

> For I would not, brethren, that ye should be ignorant of this mystery, lest ye should be wise in your own conceits; that blindness in part is happened to Israel, until the fulness of the Gentiles be come in. And so all Israel shall be saved: as it is written,

There shall come out of Zion the Deliverer, and shall turn away
ungodliness from Jacob.

(Romans 11:25–26)

In this passage, Paul was speaking of the only way in which
salvation has been, or ever will be, made available to any Israelite.
Namely, through the Deliverer Jesus Christ who came out of Zion
when he was born in 4 B.C.—over 2,000 years ago.

To harmonize with Paul's teaching elsewhere, his words, and
"so all Israel shall be saved," must be given this interpretation:
And in like manner all those of Israel predestinated and elected by
God for salvation from their sins through faith in Christ shall be
saved by the Deliverer who came out of Zion.

Isaiah the prophet also foretold this truth when he wrote these
lines in Isaiah 59:19–20:

When the enemy shall come in like a flood,
The Spirit of the Lord shall lift up a
    standard against him.
And the Redeemer shall come to Zion,
And unto them that turn from transgression
    in Jacob,
Saith the LORD.

And in Psalm 14:7, David meditated on the same truth when
he exclaimed,

Oh that the salvation of Israel were
    come out of Zion!
When the Lord bringeth back the
    captivity of his people,
Jacob shall rejoice, and Israel
    shall be glad.

Dictionary Refutes Dispensationalism

Dispensationalists interpret what Paul said in Romans 11:26 as having to do with time. That is why they make the serious mistake of interpreting Paul of saying in effect, "And at that time all Israel shall be saved by a future Deliverer." The passage in question, however, refers not to the calendar, but to the cross of Christ; Paul was speaking not about time, but about God's plan of salvation of Israelites by grace through faith in Christ the De- liverer.

Though dispensationalists hold to their time theory of Romans 11:26 and the phrase "at that time," no dictionary or lexicon con- tains those three words as a definition for the word "so." The dic- tionary definitions that give us a much better understanding of what Paul meant are these: "in that or a similar manner; in the way described; in the way indicated; often used as a substitute for a preceding clause; consequently; and therefore."[6]

The Greek word for "so" is *houtos* which means "in this way; in this manner; on this fashion; in like manner." The other defini- tions of *houtos* are "consequently" and "therefore."[7] These last two definitions deprive the dispensationalist of his time frame and re- quire him to say that all the Jews who ever lived will be saved, which he knows cannot be true because millions of Jews have died in their sins.

Using the dictionary to refute the dispensationalist's claim that the salvation described in verse 26 occurs at some future date, also refutes their use of the words, "all Israel" to describe those who are saved. "All Israel" does not refer to the salvation of every living Israelite at any given time, any more than John 1:7; 3:17; and 4:42 say that every person in the world will be saved. They read:

- "that all men through him might believe"
- "that the world through him might be saved"
- "the Saviour of the world"

---

[6]*Merriam Webster's Collegiate Dictionary* and *Oxford Canadian Dictionary.*
[7]*Greek Dictionary of the New Testament* by James Strong.

A Remnant of Jews Were Saved

Paul has already told us "that they are not all Israel which are of Israel" in Romans 9:6, so clearly he is confirming in Romans 11:26 what he has said elsewhere in his letters, namely, that a remnant of ethnic Israel will be saved through the Deliverer who came out of Zion as prophesied.

During the generation between A.D. 30 and A.D. 70 when divine judgment fell upon the Jewish nation, the Lord called and regenerated many Jews. For a Jew to come to Christ, he had to come as every other Christian Jew had come: by repenting of his sins, and believing in Jesus Christ as his Lord and Saviour.

Zion City of Our God

This is what the church believed for the first 1,800 years of its history. Here is the evidence: Paul said that the believers of his day were the Israel of God and therefore heirs to all the promises (Galatians 6:16). That has long been celebrated by the consecrated and doctrinal hymn writers of the church. For example, some 200 years ago, John Newton wrote a beautiful hymn whose opening lines came from Psalm 87:3:

Glorious things of thee are spoken,
Zion, city of our God;
He whose word cannot be broken,
Formed thee for his own abode.

In verse 3 of that hymn, Newton said he was a member of Zion's city through grace. John Newton also wrote "Amazing Grace," which has become one of the most well-known hymns of all time. We can safely say that Newton was saying in his hymns what he preached—that the glorious Zion and the eternal abode of God was not the physical city of Jerusalem, but the church of Jesus Christ. He wrote,

I love thy church O God:
Her walls before thee stand,
Dear as the apple of thine eye,
And graven on thy hand.

Those last two lines (quoted from Zechariah 2:8 and Isaiah 49:16) once referred to ethnic or national Israel, but now they apply to spiritual Israel, the church of Jesus Christ.

If the church as spiritual Israel had not replaced the nation of Israel in God's plan and purposes, believers today could lay no real claim to, or hope to spiritually profit from, the Old Testament.

Fortunately however, as John Newton and other great preachers and hymn writers of the past believed, we are Zion, the habitation of God. In the light of New Testament teaching only believers in Jesus Christ are Abraham's descendants. And the promises once given to national Israel have since been transferred to the church of our Lord Jesus Christ.

"For ye," said Paul, "are all the children of God by faith in Christ Jesus. For as many of you as have been baptized into Christ have put on Christ. There is neither Jew nor Greek, there is neither bond nor free, there is neither male nor female: for ye are all one in Christ Jesus. And if ye be Christ's, then are ye Abraham's seed, and heirs according to the promise" (Galatians 3:26–29).

God's promise to Abraham was threefold: First, the Lord promised him a new land that pointed to heaven. Second, he promised to make his posterity into a great nation that pointed to the nation or the church of Christ, which was given the kingdom and all its privileges. And third, he promised that in Abraham and his seed, all the families of the earth would be blessed. His seed was Christ "who hath abolished death, and who hath brought life and immortality to light through the gospel" (2 Timothy 1:10).

How these great redemptive blessings should move us to pray words like these from hymn writer Frances R. Havergal:

I am trusting thee, Lord Jesus,
Trusting only thee;
Trusting thee for full salvation,
Great and free.

CHAPTER NINE

WHAT WAS CHRIST'S GREATEST DECLARATION?

As soon then as he had said unto them, I am he, they went backward, and fell to the ground.

(John 18:6)

O ne day a lawyer, who was with a group of Pharisees, attempted to trap the Lord Jesus Christ with a legal question. "Master," he said, "which is the great commandment in the law?"

Knowing the lawyer's motive, Jesus said, "Thou shalt love the Lord, thy God, with all thy heart, and with all thy soul, and with all thy mind. This is the first and great commandment. And the second is like unto it, Thou shalt love thy neighbour as thyself. On these two commandments hang all the law and the prophets." (Matthew 22:36–40).

Other Views on Statements by Christ

Many might say that this response to the lawyer's question is the greatest statement ever made by Jesus Christ. Another who is missionary-minded would likely say that it was the great commission: "Go ye therefore, and teach all nations, baptizing them in the name of the Father, and of the Son, and of the Holy Ghost: teaching them to observe all things whatsoever I have commanded you: and lo, I am with you always, even unto the end of the world [age]" (Matthew 28:19–20).

Then there is the person who believes that Christ's authority is so important that he would say the greatest declaration of Christ was Matthew 28:18: "All power [authority] is given unto me in heaven and in earth."

Those who emphasize the necessity of the new birth and maintain that one must be born again before he receives the gifts of repentance and faith would likely see Christ's statement, "Except a man be born again, he cannot see the kingdom of God" as his greatest.

A minister who holds to liberal theology and the social gospel, would likely choose this statement from Christ's Sermon on the Mount: "Therefore all things whatsoever ye would that men should do to you, do ye even so to them: for this is the law and the prophets" (Matthew 7:12).

A Dramatic Scene in a Desert

The four Gospels contain many statements by Jesus Christ, all of which can be described as great, but the greatest in my judgment is made up of these two words: "I AM," which Christ made on several occasions.

First, however, let's look at a dramatic scene in a Midian desert where a shepherd is watching over his flock. The shepherd was Moses, a Hebrew who was brought up as a prince in the Egyptian court. One day when he saw an Egyptian smiting a Hebrew, he killed the Egyptian. When Pharaoh heard about it, he sought to slay Moses. But Moses escaped by fleeing to Midian, where he married and became a shepherd for his wife's father.

The Bible says that after 40 years, while Moses was watching his sheep, "the angel of the Lord appeared unto him in a flame of fire out of the midst of a bush: and he looked, and, behold, the bush burned with fire, and the bush was not consumed" (Exodus 3:2).

It was then that God called Moses to go back to Egypt and deliver the Israelites from their bondage of slavery by leading them out of Egypt. Moses asked the Lord what he should say if the Israelite slaves asked him for the name of the One who sent him to be their deliverer. After all, it was 40 years since Moses had been in Egypt, and they would wonder why they should obey one who was known to be a murderer.

God responded to Moses by saying, "I AM THAT I AM . . . Thus shalt thou say unto the children of Israel, I AM hath sent me unto you."

"I AM" is the great Jehovistic name of God. Dr. Pentecost says, "It contains each tense of the verb to be and might be translated, 'I was, I am, and I shall always continue to be.'"

Unfathomable Depth to His Name

The first thing to learn from this name is the fact that we should go forth declaring the name and nature of God as he has been revealed. No time should be wasted, and no attempts should be made to prove the existence of God. That is a self-evident truth. There is enough evidence in the created order of things to prove the eternal power and Godhead of the invisible creator God so that those who refuse to believe in him are "without excuse" (Romans 1:20).

Our business is to proclaim the name and person of God as he has revealed himself in and through Jesus Christ. There is a depth in this name which no finite mind can fathom. "I AM that I AM" announced that the great God is self-existent, beside whom there is no other god. Without beginning and without ending, he is God from everlasting to everlasting. Only God has the right to say, "I AM that I AM" because he is always the same, eternally changeless. He said, "For I am the LORD, I change not; therefore ye sons of Jacob are not consumed" (Malachi 3:6).

"I Am" Is Exclusive with God

Any man who uses "I AM" in the sense that God used it to describe himself would be a blasphemer. Paul said, "By the grace of God I am what I am." But he did not have the right to say "I am that I am." Jesus of Nazareth, however, did use it that way. Here are some of the statements he made using the words, I AM:

> "I am the door, I am the bread of Life, I am the light of the world, I am the good shepherd, I am the true vine, I am the resurrection and the life, I am the way, the truth, and the life."

Jesus Was God Incarnate

Many of the Jews thought Christ was just boasting and describing situations when he combined "I am" with "bread, life, door, shepherd, vine, light, resurrection, way" and "truth."

For this chapter, we are going to examine five occasions when Christ used the words "I AM" by themselves. The words I AM are from the Greek, *Ego Eimi,* and prove that the Lord Jesus Christ was declaring himself to be God incarnate. The Jews knew that he was calling himself God, accused him of blasphemy, and conspired together to kill Him for his claim to deity. Christ used the words "I am" with friends, enemies, sinners, and saints.

New Converts Should Begin with John

I agree with those Bible scholars who say John's gospel is the greatest book in the Bible. A new convert to Christ is wise to start reading the Bible, not with Genesis or Matthew, but with the Gospel of John. Why? Because John gives the greatest reason in the world for writing a book. "These things are written," he wrote, "that ye might believe that Jesus is the Christ, the Son of God; and that believing ye might have life through his name" (John 20:31).

John presents Jesus Christ as God repeatedly, and he reveals several things not revealed in any other book. For example, the double use of "verily" appears 25 times in the New Testament, and all of them are in John's gospel. The most poignant words of redemption, "It is finished," that Christ spoke on the cross appear only in John's gospel. Also the five occasions when the Lord Jesus called himself by "I AM"—the name of God—were reported by John alone.

CHRIST SAID, "I AM"
TO AN ADULTERESS

Christ Shows Us How to Witness

If you want to know something about personal evangelism or witnessing to unbelievers, read John's account of Jesus' encounter with the woman of Samaria at Jacob's well.[8] He began with a brilliant step-by-step explanation of the woman's sin and need.

Having listened to Jesus remove every one of her attempts to justify herself, the poor soul was ready for a revealed Saviour. She was through with trying to deceive and procrastinate. She had asked "How?" and Christ had graciously answered her (9–10). She had inquired "Whence?" and had received a kindly reply (11–14). She had brought up the subject of places of worship and Jesus told her that "God is a Spirit: and they that worship him must worship him in spirit and in truth" (20–24).

It was then that she responded to Christ by saying, "I know that Messiah cometh, which is called Christ: when he is come he will tell us all things."

"I that speak unto thee," said Jesus "am *he*."

Not in the Original Greek

The word "he" is in italics in the King James Version, which means it was not in the original Greek New Testament. Therefore what Jesus actually said was "I AM." What surprising, wonderful

---

[8]For an exposition of John as a practical manual on witnessing, see George Bowman's book, *Be Not Afraid of Their Faces*.

and amazing grace for Jesus to reveal his deity to an adulteress woman who wasn't even of the house of Israel!

That she was not some ignorant peasant was revealed in some of the things she said: she knew the history of Jacob's well (12); she knew the history of Jewish and Samaritan worship (20); and she believed in God's promise of a Messiah (25). Her accurate knowledge of the Messiah and his ability to deliver God's truth to his people, showed her to have more knowledge of Christ than many religious scholars of our day with a string of academic degrees behind their names.

CHRIST SAID, "I AM" TO HIS DISCIPLES

They Wanted a Bread-and-Fish King

The second occasion of Christ saying "I AM" is in John 6, which begins with Christ supernaturally feeding 5,000 people with a boy's lunch of five barley loaves and two small fish. Some of those who had seen this great miracle said, "This is of a truth that prophet that should come into the world."

But Jesus could read their thoughts, and he knew that they were ready to take him by force if necessary and make him their bread-and-fish king, who would feed them without their working for it. But Jesus avoided them and went up into the hills to pray, while his disciples went down to the Sea of Galilee, boarded a ship, and headed for Capernaum.

Jesus Was Not with Them

It is quite probable that they shared their thoughts about the great miracle they had seen and the 12 baskets that were filled with leftovers! Like the multitude who had been fed, they likely reasoned that Jesus was that prophet whose coming had been promised in the Old Testament.

As they rowed their boat, a strong wind suddenly rose, and they found themselves in the midst of a raging storm that, in spite of their experience as sailors and fishermen, made it difficult to row. Matthew said they were being tossed, Mark said they were toiling, and John said the sea arose and the wind blew and Jesus was not with them.

What Manner of Man Is This?

Seasoned sailors that they were, they were afraid. In an earlier storm, they were also afraid, but Jesus, who was asleep in the stern, was in the boat with them. Thinking they were going to drown, they woke Jesus, who rose and commanded the storm to be still.

When they saw the great calm that came over the waters, the disciples said, "What manner of man is this, that even the wind and the sea obey him?" (Mark 4:37–41).

Oh, the Hardness of the Human Heart!

In the second storm, however, they couldn't ask for Jesus' help because he was not in the ship with them. After rowing about three miles, they saw Jesus in the midst of the storm walking on the water. Matthew and Mark said they were troubled and cried out in fear thinking that Jesus was a ghost or spirit. John said they were afraid, but Jesus said to them, "It is I; be not afraid." When rightly translated, these words would read, "Be not afraid, I AM."

Having heard Jesus speak, Peter tried to go to the Lord, walking on the water. When he looked around at the crashing waves, he began to sink. "Lord," he cried, "save me!" (Matthew 14:30). Christ then demonstrated that he was the great I AM by stretching forth his hand and pulling Peter to safety. Matthew said that when Jesus and Peter got into the boat, all the disciples worshiped him.

In Mark's account, he said that the disciples "were sore amazed in themselves beyond measure, and wondered. For they considered not the miracle of the loaves; for their heart was hardened" (Mark 6:51–52). Oh, the hardness of the human heart! In spite of seeing the miracle of feeding the 5,000, seeing him walking on the water, and hearing his statement, "I AM," they didn't believe in his deity!

CHRIST SAID "I AM" TO HIS ENEMIES

They Were No Match for Jesus

Jesus had many enemies among the Jewish leaders who constantly tried to trap him into saying something to support their false accusations against him. But they were no match for him. Christ verbally defeated them every time, until they became so frustrated they conspired to get rid of him by having him put to death.

In verses 37 and 40 of John 8, Jesus said that they were seeking to kill him; in verse 48 his enemies said he was a Samaritan and had a devil, and in verse 53 they asked him point blank, "Art thou greater than our father Abraham, which is dead?"

Not "I Am He," But "I AM."

Three times in the same chapter, the Lord Jesus Christ said, "I AM" to those enemies. In verse 24, Christ said, "Ye shall die in your sins: for if ye believe not that I AM *he*, ye shall die in your sins." In verse 28, he said to them, "When ye have lifted up the Son of man, then shall ye know that I AM *he*, and that I do nothing of myself; but as my Father hath taught me, I speak these things."

The King James Version printed the word "he" in italics for both verses, which means the word was not in the original. So instead of Christ saying, "I am he," he was saying "I AM," the very words the Lord used in identifying himself to Moses. For Jesus to say "I AM" was the same as saying, "I am God."

Continuing Hostility Toward Christ

John 8:58 records the 3rd time that the Lord Jesus applied the great Jehovistic name of God to himself. Speaking to the adversarial scribes and Pharisees who questioned his words about Abraham being glad about seeing Christ's day, Jesus said, "Verily, verily, I say unto you, Before Abraham was, I am."

There is no doubt that the Jews knew what he was doing and saying. He was claiming to be alive before Abraham was born, which meant he was claiming to be God. That declaration by Christ made the scribes and Pharisees furious. "Then took they up stones to cast at him: but Jesus hid himself, and went out of the temple, going through the midst of them, and so passed by" (John 8:59).

The hostility and enmity against the deity and person of Christ is just as prevalent today as it was 2,000 years ago. The false cults make it a point to regularly attack the biblical truth of the deity of Christ. For example, here are what different cults say on this subject:

- *Jehovah Witnesses* deny Christ's deity by saying, "Jesus Christ was a man—neither more nor less."
- *Christian Scientists* deny Christ's deity when they say, "Jesus Christ is not God as he is said to have declared."
- *Mormonism* is subtle in their denial of Christ's deity. "The Father," they say, "has begotten him in his own likeness. Who is the Father? He is the first of the human family."
- *Theosophy* also insults the Lord by saying, "Jesus gave to the world fragments of teaching of value as basis for world religion, as did men like Buddha, Confucius, Plato, Pythagoras, etc."
- *Modern or Liberal Theology* calls itself a Christian religion, but shows itself to be an enemy of Christ when it says, "Jesus Christ is an idyllic figure, the flower of humanity, the world's greatest ethical teacher. A man so good that his deluded followers took him for a god."

- *Spiritualism* calls Christ a liar when it says, "Christ himself was nothing more than a medium of high order . . . Jesus Christ was not divine . . . He never claimed to be God manifest in the flesh."
- *Eastern Mysticism* tries to go ecumenical by saying, "All religions from times immemorial are just different branches of the main trunk of the eternal religion represented by the Vedas. Christ is considered to be one of a long line of 'Masters' who had themselves realized divinity . . . His picture is frequently to be seen beside that of Buddha, or of Shankaracharya, or of Yogananda, or other recognized Divine leaders."⁹
- *Islam:* "Christ Jesus the son of Mary was no more than a messenger of Allah . . . Do not say 'Trinity': desist: it will be better for you: for Allah is one God: Glory be to Him: for exalted is he above having a son" (Qur'an Surah 4:171).

It is obvious that most men and women do not accept Christ's equality with God the Father and reject the doctrine of the Trinity. Though Islam teaches that Christ was a great prophet, it also says, "Fight and slay the pagans [any who disagree with Islam] wherever you find them, seize them, beleaguer them, and lie in wait for them in every stratagem of war" (Qur'an Surah 9:29). Sounds like the battle cry for terrorists!

Such hostility and opposition of false religions to Christ and his people should not be a surprise to us. The history of Christianity is laced with their persecution, cruelty, and murder of believers in Christ as God the Son. "They hated me," said Jesus, "without a cause" (John 15:25). And to his disciples, he said, "In the world ye shall have tribulation" (John 16:33).

Such persecutors will not escape their just punishment from the Lord. As one preacher put it, "There will be a payday someday!" The Jewish persecutors of the early Christians were pun-

⁹Taken from the pamphlet, *The Spirit of Truth and the Spirit of Error* by Keith L. Brooks and revised by Irvine Robertson (Chicago: Moody Bible Institute, 1976).

ished by the Lord when he came, not visibly, but in judgment in A.D. 67–70. At that time he used the Roman armies to put an end to the rebellious Jewish nation, abolish their apostate religion, destroy their capital city of Jerusalem, and raze and burn their temple. It was a watershed event of history.

CHRIST SAID "I AM" CONCERNING HIS BETRAYAL

Prophecy Proves Christ's Deity

In the 13th chapter of John's gospel, we have a plain statement that the great "I AM" knows all things and predicted exactly what would happen concerning his betrayal, trial, crucifixion, and resurrection.

"I speak not of you all: I know whom I have chosen: but that the scripture may be fulfilled, He that eateth bread with me hath lifted up his heel against me. Now I tell you before it come, that, when it is come to pass, ye may believe that I am *he*" (John 13:18, 19). Again the word "he" is in italics because it was not in the original.

This passage shows that the prophetic scriptures were not given to man to satiate his curiosity, but to glorify the Godhead: God the Father, God the Son, and God the Holy Spirit. They were also given and fulfilled that we may believe that Christ is the great I AM.

Inner and Outer Darkness

Although we are told later in verse 28 that the apostles did not know that Judas Iscariot was the betrayer, many years after the incident when John wrote his divinely-inspired gospel he wrote, "He [Judas Iscariot] then having received the sop went immediately out: and it was night" (John 13:30).

And what a night it was for Judas! He went out into the darkness of the night outside, but the darkness of the night inside his spirit was the darkness of perdition. He had chosen to take the road that took him to destruction. When he discovered that the Jewish leaders had used him in their plan to murder Christ, he went back to them in the temple and, flinging the 30 pieces of silver he had been given by them for betraying Christ, he said, "I have betrayed the innocent blood!" Then he went out and hanged himself.

How sad that there are so many millions of sinners who continue to betray Christ by the evil lusts of their minds, the wicked actions of their lives, and the blasphemous words of their mouths. Like the murderers of Christ, they yell, "We will not have this man to rule over us!" They reject the great I AM. Like Judas they have a darkness of spirit that, unless they are converted, will take them in the same direction as Judas took to a place that Jesus described as "outer darkness. There shall be weeping and gnashing of teeth" (Matthew 8:12).

CHRIST SAID "I AM" WHEN HE WAS ARRESTED

The Scene at Gethsemane

Judas Iscariot had heard the Lord Jesus declare that he was the great I AM in the upper room at the Last Supper (John 13:19). But it had no affect on Judas. He even heard the same words twice more before he went out and hanged himself. John 18 says that Judas and a band of armed Jewish officers and authorities, sent by the chief priests and Pharisees, came to arrest Jesus in the garden of Gethsemane where he and his apostles had gone to pray. The record says that Jesus, knowing what was about to happen to him, went toward the band of men and Judas.

"Whom seek ye?" he asked.

"Jesus of Nazareth," they said.

"I am *he*," he said.

Again the word "he" is in italics indicating that it was not included in the original. Therefore Christ was saying, "I AM," to the men and Judas. When Christ said, "I AM," all the men fell backward to the ground.

As the I AM, he had the power to prevent those wicked men from arresting, torturing, and killing him. The armed band, prostrate and helpless on the ground before him, were completely at his mercy. It would have been a simple thing for him to walk away. It was a display of Christ's divine majesty and the power of his word. He did not strike anyone with his hands because there was no need for physical force. After all, he created the universe with the power of his word. All he had to do was speak two monosyllables, and all those armed men were completely overcome.

Why Jesus Used the Divine Force of I AM

Why did Jesus use the power of the words I AM to overcome those who had come to arrest him?

First, he wanted to show that he was more than "Jesus of Nazareth." The Jews who heard him would know the divine meaning of the words I AM.

Second, he wanted to demonstrate that they had no power to either arrest, torture, or kill him unless he allowed them to do so.

Third, it left those wicked men without excuse for their opposition to Christ. They weren't machines, but men who were responsible for their actions. One wonders at the ignorance and wicked boldness they displayed to get up off the ground and put their hands on Jesus who had displayed such power over them! The only answer is unbelief and lack of fear. They did not believe Jesus was God, and "they had no fear of God before their eyes" (Romans 3:18).

Part of God's Redemptive Plan

Christ allowed them to arrest him, because it was an essential part of God's plan to redeem a people for himself that Christ do nothing to prevent his arrest. He was to offer himself as the Lamb of God—a vicarious sacrifice to meet all the penal demands of God's law on behalf of his elect people.

It appears that Christ did not perceive the armed men who came to arrest him as his elect. In dealing with them, he never employed the tenderness he used with the Samaritan woman at Jacob's well. Though he used the words "I AM" with her, he used them to lead her to true faith in him.

The armed men were not convinced that he was the Messiah. Here is an illustration of the triumph of divine truth in those who are saved and in those who perish. Paul felt this way about the apostles' ministry for he wrote, "For we are unto God a sweet savour of Christ, in them that are saved, and in them that perish: To the one we are the savour of death unto death; and to the other the savour of life unto life" (2 Corinthians 2:15–16).

The Power to Provide Every Need

Jesus gave a beautiful summation of his "I AM" title in his directives to John about writing the last book of the Bible. "I am Alpha and Omega, the beginning and the ending, saith the Lord, which is, and which was, and which is to come, the Almighty" (Revelation 1:8).

Alpha is the first letter in the Greek alphabet, and Omega is the last letter. The Lord Jesus Christ is not only the first and the last letter of the alphabet, but all the holy literature in between. When Christ called himself "I AM," it was like saying to his own people that he had the power to provide their every need. "Ask," he said, "and it shall be given unto you; seek, and ye shall find; knock, and it shall be opened unto you" (Matthew 7:7).

It is like Jesus giving us a blank check for us to make out in the amount necessary to provide everything we need to live in loving obedience to his precepts. Every one of us needs life. Christ says, "I AM the Life." Every one of us needs righteousness. He is "the Lord our Righteousness." We need peace with God. The Bible says that "he is our peace." There is no victory in this life unless we have wisdom, sanctification, and redemption. The Bible says that he is made all three unto us (1 Corinthians 1:30).

Some of the I AM Riches in Christ

It would take a trip through the wide range of human necessities to gain an accurate conception of the amazing depth and fullness of "I AM"—the greatest declaration Christ ever made. It is a profound and blessed name that calls for our praise, adoration, thankfulness, and devotion to his glorious cause. To conclude this chapter, here are some of the riches in that glorious title:

- Are you spiritually hungry? Jesus says, "I AM the bread of life."
- Are you in the darkness of doubt? Jesus says, "I AM the light of the world."
- Are you groping for spiritual direction? Jesus says, "I AM the way."
- Are you looking for a door that leads to redemptive blessings? Jesus says, "I AM the door."
- Are you in need of spiritual sustenance? Jesus says, "I AM the life."
- Are you looking for right answers to life's many questions? Jesus says, "I AM the truth."
- Does your life seem to be like a plant that does not bear fruit? Jesus says, "I AM the vine, ye are the branches: He that abideth in me, and I in him, the same bringeth forth much fruit: for without me ye can do nothing."
- Do you know you need a substitute? Jesus said, "I AM the good shepherd: the good shepherd giveth his life for the sheep."
- Do you want to see your Christian loved ones who have died and gone to heaven? Jesus says, "I AM the resurrection, and the life: he that believeth in me, though he were dead, yet shall he live."

CHAPTER TEN

ARE YOU HAPPY?

Blessed is the man that walketh not in the counsel of the un-godly, nor standeth in the way of sinners, nor sitteth in the seat of the scornful.

(Psalm 1:1)

Though most men and women have a great desire to be happy, they have the wrong idea of what happiness is all about. They believe that happiness depends upon happenings in their lives. They try to find happiness in wealth, pleasure, accomplishments, and good health. But that cannot be true because many rich, successful and healthy people are miserable, and some have even committed suicide.

Jesus warned against trying to find happiness in possessions when he said, "Take heed, and beware of covetousness: for a man's life consisteth not in the abundance of the things he possesseth" (Luke 12:15).

I Thought I Was Happy

Webster's dictionary defines happiness as, "Good luck, good fortune; prosperity, a state of well-being, graceful aptitude." But happiness can be elusive, counterfeited, and misrepresented. Here, for example, is evidence of the truth of that statement from my own life:

In my teens and early twenties, I thought I was happy. In high school I was on the honor roll, played varsity football and was chosen for the All-State team. In addition, I was active in the drama society and took part in the junior and senior plays. In college, more of what I thought were happy-making honors followed.

I was elected president of my junior class and again in my senior year. Involved in the varsity football and track teams, I was also president of the drama club, and had lead parts in the junior and senior plays. At the same time, I was dating a beauty queen. But much of this accomplishment was a counterfeit for happiness, because I know there were times when deep down in my heart I had to admit I wasn't really happy at all. I learned that it is easy to substitute achievements and accomplishments for happiness.

My pride was also bolstered by the fact that I did not drink or smoke. Sometimes on weekends at fraternity affairs, I would be the only sober person present. One activity in my life, however, robbed me of any happiness I thought I had. I loved to gamble and would spend long hours at night trying to beat the odds. But many times I returned to my room in the early morning hours counting my losses instead of winnings. I knew I was not happy.

Christ's Water of Life

Reflecting back on some of those unsatisfying, sinful college days, now that I am a Christian, I often think of the conversation that Jesus had with the woman whom he met at Jacob's well in Samaria, "Whosoever drinketh of this water," he said, "shall thirst again" (John 4:13).

He meant that the temporary cisterns of this world cannot provide any lasting satisfaction or happiness. Jesus told the woman about what she needed to provide lasting satisfaction. "But whosoever drinketh of the water that I shall give him," he said, "shall never thirst; but the water that I shall give him shall be in him a well of water springing up into everlasting life" (John 4:14).

I Found True Happiness in the Woods

After a football injury in the fall of 1941, and six months of nervous breakdown, depression, and confinement that led me to attempt suicide, I felt that my life was without hope. On Easter Sunday, 1942, I walked a half a mile from my home into the woods and open fields, fell on my knees and prayed. Calling on God, I confessed my sins, and asked him to forgive me, save me, and help me.

That Easter afternoon, I not only received the gift of salvation and forgiveness, but I discovered the nature of true happiness. Ever since that April afternoon I've been happy, really happy. I now find happiness in every area of my life. I am happy in my work, in my home, with my wife, with my children, and with my grandchildren. And especially am I happy because I know the One who is the source of all happiness. I'm sure that is exactly what God wants in all his children.

The Formula for Happiness

I believe the Lord gives the formula for happiness in the first Psalm, which begins with these words: "Blessed is the man . . ." The word "blessed" means "most fortunate and happy," so some Bible translations read "Happy is the man . . ."

This is in keeping with the dictionary definition for "blessed," which is "to make happy." The subject of happiness is so important that God has recorded in Jeremiah 17:7–8 much the same words as David wrote in Psalm 1.

"Blessed is the man that trusteth in the LORD," wrote Jeremiah, "and whose hope the LORD is. For he shall be as a tree planted by the waters, and that spreadeth out her roots by the river, and shall not see when heat cometh, but her leaf shall be green; and shall not be careful in the year of drought, Neither shall cease from yielding fruit."

What is the formula for happiness? You can know that formula by learning these three elements of happiness: separation, sustenance, and success.

HAPPINESS IS SEPARATION

Negative Statements

God's way of presenting how one can be happy might come as a surprise, a disappointment, or even a shock to some people. The happy man, says Psalm 1, is one whose life is marked by things he should abstain and avoid. The psalm actually opens with these three negative statements. "Blessed is the man that walketh not in the counsel of the ungodly, nor standeth in the way of sinners, nor sitteth in the seat of the scornful."

One might ask, "How can three negatives contribute to such a positive condition of heart as happiness?" Like every other worthwhile possession, happiness is a goal to gain by overcoming obstacles. It is a victory worth fighting for. Psalm 1 is a beatitude, not for a person who is lazy, but for one who is determined. There is no getting away from the fact that behind the serenity of the saints is a personal struggle to overcome the negatives of life.

Separation and Blessing Go Together

The three negative statements in Psalm 1 pertain to man's very existence, for they speak of walking, sitting, and standing in ways that are separate from the world of unbelief and wickedness. David was not alone in writing about separation.

Many years before David was born, the Lord commanded Abram (later called "Abraham") to separate himself from where he lived as part of God's plan to redeem a people for himself. "Get thee out of thy country," the Lord told him, "and from thy kindred, and from thy father's house, unto a land I will show thee; And I will make of thee a great nation, and I will bless thee, and make thy name great; and thou shalt be a blessing" (Genesis 12:1–2).

We cannot help but notice in these words that there is a vital connection between separation and blessing or happiness. It was only by Abraham separating himself as directed by God that he would find happiness and be used to bless others.

Later there was much strife between Abraham's herdsmen and the herdsmen working for his nephew Lot. God said that separation was the only way to settle their differences. After Lot and his herdsmen with their cattle separated from Abraham, the Lord said to Abraham, "Lift up now thine eyes, and look from the place where thou art for all the land which thou seest, to thee will I give it, and to thy seed forever" (Genesis 13:14–15).

Separation According to Moses and Solomon

God commanded his people Israel to separate themselves from the pagan nations in the then-known world. In a prayer to God, Moses said that they would be known as having found grace in God's sight because he was with them and they were separated "from all the people that are upon the face of the earth" (Exodus 33:16).

One of the most God-honoring prayers in the Bible, Solomon's prayer to dedicate the temple has this principle of God separating Israel from pagan peoples to be his inheritance. In that prayer, Solomon also spoke of how the Lord delivered the Israelites from slavery by separating them from the nation of Egypt (1 Kings 8:53).

Paul's Explanation of Separation

The apostles taught the doctrine of separation to the early Christians. Believers were called saints, which meant they were sanctified by the Holy Spirit who set them aside for God's holy use. He also provided them with his presence and power to help them live a separated life by progressing in holiness. One of the best passages on the subject is in 2 Corinthians 6, where Paul wrote these pregnant words:

Be ye not unequally yoked together with unbelievers: for what fellowship hath righteousness with unrighteousness? and what communion hath light with darkness? And what concord hath Christ with Belial? or what part hath he that believeth with an infidel?

Paul then gives his reason why Christians should live separate from the world of wickedness and false religions:

> And what agreement hath the temple of God with idols? For ye are the temple of the living God; as God hath said, I will dwell in them and walk in them; and I will be their God and they shall be my people.

As he continued to teach this doctrine of separation, Paul went on to exhort the believers on what God says they should do in order to apply this principle of separation to their own lives. He said,

> Wherefore come out from among them, and be ye separate, saith the Lord, and touch not the unclean thing; and I will receive you, and be a Father unto you, and ye shall be my sons and daughters, saith the Lord Almighty.

The Ungodly Are Practical Atheists

The man who would make a real success of his life, the man who desires to be genuinely happy, must as David said, "Walketh not in the counsel of the ungodly." Such a man refuses to take direction from the ungodly. In our attempt to find blessing or happiness by refusing to walk according to the advice given by the ungodly, we must learn to identify the ungodly.

The ungodly are those persons who strive to be autonomous, which means wanting to be "a law unto themselves." God and his holy laws mean nothing to them. They love to live and reckon with no thought of God. They do not have to be drunkards or libertines.

The ungodly man can a be decent, respectable person in the eyes of society, but he makes a practice of deliberate ignorance when it comes to the truth that God has the right to call him to give account of what he has done with the life God gave him. The ungodly could be classified as the practical atheists of our day.

Advice Without Experience

What effective advice can the ungodly, sinful, and scorners give us? None at all! If we want profitable advice and wise direction, we are better to seek it from those who do not walk with the ungodly, stand with sinners, and sit with the scornful.

If it were not so sad, it would be amusing to read newspaper columns offering advice to the lovelorn. In many cases they are written by those whose lives show nothing of the advice they give to others. Some of them have failed in their own marriages. It is amazing how many unqualified people there are who are quick to give advice. You can meet them in churches, offices, hospitals, or while traveling on a plane.

Sin Has Only One Direction: Downward

The man who would be genuinely happy must refuse to stand in the way of sinners. Standing in the way of sinners puts one in a lower level spiritually from walking in the counsel of the ungodly. The man who is walking may still have the ability to keep going when tempted to sin. But to stop and stand in the way or company of sinners manifests an interest in enjoying some sinful pleasure. It indicates that one is increasing his propensity to do evil as though he was falling under its spell. Sin has only one direction: downward. It is amazing what great evils can grow from even a small interest in sin.

For example, one day a friend who was visiting the preacher, Dr. Wilbur Chapman, showed him some small seeds and asked, "From what kind of a plant would you say these seeds came?"

"I should think," said Dr. Chapman, "they came from one that was very small indeed." "No, you are mistaken," said his friend; "these small seeds came from a plant that is 300 ft. high, 35 ft. in diameter, and 105 ft. in circumference."

He was referring to the giant redwood tree of California. The most impressive fact about redwood seeds is their tremendous growing power. It is the same with sin. How easy it is for a small evil desire to grow into a giant act of wickedness! When we make an analysis of sin, we find that one must make four distinctive steps or go through four stages to commit sin. Those stages are look, covet, take, and hide, which were evident in the sin of Eve. The Bible says that she "saw that the tree was good for food, and that it was pleasant to the eyes, and a tree to be desired to make one wise, she took of the fruit thereof and did eat." Later she and Adam hid themselves (Genesis 3:6, 8).

How easy it is to change one's moral posture from walking with the ungodly to standing in the way of sinners!

The daily news media present concrete evidence that the morals of men and women are on a steep decline. More and more of what we called evil some years ago is growing in social acceptance. For example, some governments are talking about legalizing the use of drugs, homosexual perversion, and prostitution. One prostitute who got into a stranger's car and offered sex for money was declared innocent of any wrongdoing by the Supreme Court of Canada! It seems to be the tendency of human nature to increase its visits to the slippery slopes of moral decline.

HAPPINESS IS SUSTENANCE

Reading the Word of God with the Right Attitude

Some might think that it would be impossible to find happiness by reading the Bible. "That ancient book is too boring to read," they say. "What pleasure could one find in reading it?" The happy man of God, however, disagrees with that opinion, because the Bible says "his delight is in the law [or Word] of the LORD; and in his law doth he meditate day and night."

So finding happiness in reading the Bible depends on one's spiritual posture. If he refuses to take advice from the ungodly, avoids the company of sinners, and does not enjoy the fellowship of the scornful, he will delight in the Word of God and will not be able to get enough of it.

It is only by reading the Bible with a right attitude that one could find delight in it. Some attend church, take a liberal approach to the Bible and accuse conservatives of interpreting the Bible literally. These two positions have been in conflict for centuries. But neglect of the Bible is worse than either a liberal or literal view of the Bible. And yet thousands of people are guilty of it.

The Bible warns about the sin of neglecting its great redemptive truth. "How shall we escape," it says, "if we neglect so great salvation; which at the first began to be spoken by the Lord, and was confirmed unto us by them that heard him?" (Hebrews 2:3).

The spiritual profit offered the reader of the Bible is lost to one who neglects to read it. It may lie on the coffee table or night table, but it has no value while it lies unread. Why read the Bible? There are many reasons:

The Bible shows us how to escape our sin through faith in Christ. The only authoritative place to find out anything about Christ is in the Bible—especially in the Gospels where Jesus said, "for God so loved the world, that he gave his only begotten Son, that whosoever believeth in him should not perish, but have everlasting life" (John 3:16).

And Peter showed the exclusiveness of Christ when he said, "Neither is there salvation in any other: for there is none other name under heaven given among men, whereby we must be saved" (Acts 4:12).

The Bible has the truth about many subjects. It has the only reliable account of the origin of life and the creation of the universe. It is the only reliable history book in print. It explains the reason and only cure for sin. No other legal textbook presents such a simple and inclusive system of law as does the Bible. It teaches more true psychology than is taught in all secular textbooks on the subject.

Have you ever asked yourself, "How did all the animals and birds get their names?" The Bible gives the answer in Genesis 2:19. There it says that God brought all the animals and birds he had created to "Adam to see what he would call them: and whatsoever Adam called every living creature, that was the name thereof."

Are you interested in astronomy? Read Job 38. If you are taken up with prophecy, the Bible has hundreds of prophecies and the record of many of them being fulfilled. Honest teachers of English literature present the Bible as the literary classic of all.

The Bible quickens the mind. A man never feels so small as when strolling among the alpine mountains of God's eternal Word. Though the reader will find the Bible answers many questions, he will never be able to exhaustively grasp its contents. The vast themes of the Bible have challenged the greatest minds in the world.

The blessed and happy man not only reads his Bible, he delights in its contents. He also finds it contains many directives on how to live and do those things that please God. He delights in the Bible because he delights in the Lord. Reading the Bible, he finds it to be satisfying, but never tires of going back for more. And the more he reads, the greater his delight.

HAPPINESS IS SUCCESS

Personal Prosperity

David used three similes to describe the blessed or happy man who refuses to walk with the ungodly, stand with sinners, and sit with the scornful. He likened him to a tree, its fruit, and its leaves.

> And he shall be like a tree planted by the rivers of water, that bringeth forth his fruit in his season; his leaf also shall not wither; and whatsoever he doeth shall prosper.
>
> (Psalm 1:3)

The happy man is not the one who necessarily is successful as the winner of things. According to the original, David did not say, "and whatsoever he doeth shall prosper." A better translation reads, "In whatsoever he doeth he shall prosper."

The Christian does not always prosper materially. I have known some very good men who were materially poor, but spiritually rich. David meant that the man who delights in God and his Word shall enjoy spiritual prosperity in all he does in every area of his life.

Joseph, the son of Jacob, who was so badly treated by his brothers, was a godly man who prospered in spite of all the opposition and false charges brought against him. But his prosperity was not merely in his change of residence from a nomad's tent to the Egyptian palace on the Nile. If that was the only prosperity he enjoyed, it likely would have worked to his everlasting ruin. His real prosperity was not in what he had gained, but in who he was.

For example, when a beautiful married woman tempted him to engage in the sinful pleasures of adultery, he said, "How then can I do this great wickedness and sin against God?"

A Happy Man Is Like a Tree Planted

According to David, the happy man will be "like a tree planted by the rivers of water." Trees are one of the most beautiful, profitable, and effective parts of God's creation. They provide a dwelling place for birds, shade from the sun, fruit for men and beast, and make a major contribution to conservation. They help to conserve soil and water. They prevent topsoil from being blown away.

The *World Book* says, "Trees help preserve the balance of gases in the atmosphere. A tree's leaves absorb carbon dioxide from the air. They also produce oxygen and release it into the atmosphere. These two processes are necessary for people to live. People could not survive if the air had too much carbon dioxide or too little oxygen."

Obviously, God made trees to be instruments of his for good to man, beast, birds, and the atmosphere. The man of God who has learned how to live for him is also an influence for good and the gospel where God has planted him.

David's use of the word "planted" implies purpose. The tree he wrote about was not there by mere chance—it was planted. A planted tree is a picture of the man God uses in his service. He is chosen and planted or placed where God intends to use him. A happy man is like a tree planted that weathers the storms that blow—a picture of stability and steadfastness. He refuses to be "tossed to and fro, and carried about with every wind of doctrine, by the sleight of men, and cunning craftiness, whereby they lie in wait to deceive" (Ephesians 4:14).

God give us men. The time demands
Strong minds, great hearts, true faith,
    And willing hands.
Men whom the lust of office does not kill;
Men whom the spoils of office cannot buy;
Men who possess an opinion and a will;
Men who have honor; men who will not lie.

The Happy Man Is Like a Fruitful Tree

The happy man is rich in usefulness. Like David's tree, "He bringeth forth his fruit in his season." A fruit tree provides sustenance for the hungry, and the happy man in Christ should be like a fruitful tree, well rooted in the Word and providing spiritual sustenance for others.

The Christian's fruit is not, as some say, the number of souls he wins to Christ. Modern evangelists often talk about converts to faith in Christ as the fruit of their ministry. Many missionaries, pastors, and Sunday school teachers do the same. Those who exercise repentance and faith in Christ are not the fruit of the Lord's servants, but of the Holy Spirit.

For one thing, it is impossible to win a soul to Christ or to persuade one to change from being spiritually dead in sin to a new creation in Christ. That is the prerogative of God the Holy Spirit. No one can go to Christ for salvation, unless the Father draws him by his Spirit and the new birth.

The Christian's fruit has to do with the way he thinks, acts and speaks. Called the fruit of the Holy Spirit, it is a singular fruit with nine sections to it. Here is a table to show the nine sections of the fruit of the Spirit and their unity:

LOVE	JOY	PEACE
PATIENCE	KINDNESS	GOODNESS
FAITHFULNESS	GENTLENESS	SELF-CONTROL

Since it is one fruit with nine sections, it would be impossible to manifest the fruit of the Spirit in one's life unless he put to practice all nine sections. In fact, they go together, for one could not exercise patience, for example, if he was not a loving, joyful, peaceful, kind, good, faithful, gentle, and self-controlled person. The exercise of any one section of the fruit requires the other eight sections to be in place.

The Happy Man Is Like a Tree Whose Leaves Do Not Wither

The happy man is happy because he has the life that abides. "His leaf also shall not wither." True men of God who delight in his Word are like evergreen trees. Pine trees, for example, manifest a year-round beauty, and for that reason many people plant them around their homes. The pine is not as brilliant as a maple or many other trees bursting in colorful autumn foliage.

After the other trees drop their leaves in the fall, however, there stands the pine tree as beautiful as ever. When the winter snows come, the pine takes the snow and beautifies it with its green needles while the rest of the trees are drab, stark naked and have retreated to months of barrenness.

A tree whose leaves do not wither is also a good picture of the happy man in Christ who maintains a consistent testimony to the grace of God in his life. Even if a fruit tree has no fruit on it, it can be identified by its leaves. Every Christian should be like that— radiating his identification with Christ by how he lives and speaks at all times and in every kind of circumstance.

Making a Right Value Comparison

Psalm 1 has six verses. The first three describe the godly man who is blessed or happy. The last three describe the ungodly man. David said the ungodly man is like the chaff that the wind blows away. He will never be able to defend himself before the divine tribunal. He cannot enjoy the fellowship of the righteous. And he is on a disaster route because "the way of the ungodly shall perish."

What a contrast!

Christ also described the ungodly man when he said, "What shall it profit a man, if he shall gain the whole world, and lose his own soul" (Mark 8:36). In these words, Christ made a right value comparison between the man who has been saved from his sins and on his way to heaven, and the man who has gained all the popularity, power and prosperity of the world, only to perish in his sins.

The Tragedy of Mark Twain

Mark Twain, one of America's famous authors (whose real name was Samuel Clemens), was like the ungodly man of Psalm 1. Born in Missouri along the Mississippi River in 1835, he died in 1910. Before he became an author, he served as a steamboat captain on the Mississippi and in the cavalry of the Confederate army during the American Civil War. His popular books included Tom *Sawyer, Huckleberry Finn, The Prince and the Pauper,* and *Life on the Mississippi.* Though his wife was a Christian who witnessed to him many times, he persistently rejected the gospel. Before he died in 1910, he wrote this morbid piece:

> A myriad of men are born; they labor and sweat and struggle for bread; they squabble and scold and fight; they scramble for little mean advantages over each other; age creeps upon them; infirmities follow; shames and humiliations bring down their prides and their vanities; those they love are taken from them, and the joy of life is turned to aching grief. The burden of pain, care, and misery grows heavier year by year; at length ambition is dead; pride is dead; vanity is dead; longing for release is in their place. It comes at last, the only unpoisoned gift earth ever had for them, they vanish from a world where they were of no consequence, where they achieved nothing, where they were a mistake and a failure and a foolishness; where they left no sign that

they have existed, a world which will lament them a day and forget them forever.

With all of his talent for writing, his popularity, and fame, Mark Twain was not like the blessed and happy man of Psalm 1:1–3, but more like the ungodly man of Psalm 1:4–6. His litany of negatives above is the testimony of an unbeliever who walked in the counsel of the ungodly, stood in the way of sinners, and sat in the seat of the scornful!

He must have owned a Bible, but obviously, his delight was not in the reading of it, and he did not meditate in it day and night because he lived and died as an atheist. He was not like David's fruitful tree that was planted deep in the good earth bringing forth fruit and manifesting leaves that never wither.

And, though he prospered financially and was a very famous author, he himself did not prosper in the true and eternal and spiritual riches that can be found exclusively in a right, grace-and-faith relationship with Jesus Christ. Mark Twain's writings show that he was an intelligent man with an unusual ability to communicate.

His readers often called him a great man; but the Bible says that all great men are not wise, and Mark Twain's ideas about religion bore evidence of the truth of that biblical statement. He enjoyed the fame and popularity and prosperity of a great writer, but he did not have the wisdom that comes from a fear of God. What a tragedy was Mark Twain! With all of his learning, pleasures, possessions, fame, and personal power, his life was an existence without meaning, without purpose, and without true happiness because he lived it with no desire to be right with God.

David closes the first psalm by showing the vivid contrast between the righteous in Christ and those who reject him. "For the LORD knoweth the way of the righteous," he wrote, "but the way of the ungodly shall perish" (Psalm 1:6).

CHAPTER ELEVEN

WHAT IS LIFE'S GREATEST TRUTH?

Verily, verily, I say unto thee, Except a man be born of water and of the Spirit, he cannot enter into the kingdom of God.

(John 3:5)

During Dwight L. Moody's evangelistic campaign in the city of St. Louis, a man named Valentine Burke was converted to faith in Christ. Though likely named after Saint Valentine, his former life was not patterned after that famous martyr of Christianity. He had been a crook and a robber.

After his conversion, Burke went to New York City to find work. Finding only temporary work, he returned to his home city of St. Louis. Upon his arrival, he received a summons from the sheriff's office that he was wanted at the court house.

Burke obeyed with a heavy heart. "Some old case they have against me," he said, "but, if I'm guilty I'll tell them the truth, I'm done lying."

The sheriff smiled and greeted him with kindness. "Where have you been Burke?"

"In New York."

"What have you been doing there?"

"Trying to find a decent job."

"Have you kept a good grip on the religion you told me about?"

Looking steadily at the sheriff, Burke said, "Yes. I've had a hard time, Sheriff, but I haven't lost my religion."

"Burke," said the sheriff, "I've had you shadowed every day you were in New York. I thought your religion was a fraud, a fake, a trick. But I must confess that I know you have lived an honest life, you went to church and did not do one thing that would betray your Christian profession. I have sent for you to offer you a deputyship under me, and you can begin at once."

Valentine Burke, the former burglar and thief, set his face like flint. Steadily and with dogged faithfulness, the former thief went about his duties until many in St. Louis began to talk about his usefulness to the police force.

Years after Burke's conversion, Moody was passing through St. Louis and received a call to meet his convert at one of the upper rooms of the court house. Moody told how he found Valentine Burke sitting at a table guarding a sack of diamonds worth more than $70,000.

Knowing that God had used Moody to show him the way of salvation and the power of a new changed life, Burke said, "Mr. Moody, see what the grace of God can do for a burglar. Look at this: The sheriff picked me out of all his men to guard this bag of jewels."

Regeneration, or the new birth, had made Burke the crook into a changed man. Most people do not realize why regeneration is so important. Unless one is regenerated, however, he has no hope for the future. He might have a few more months or years to live here, but then his death will rob him of all opportunity of getting right with God. Looking back on his short life, he will realize that all of those sinful pleasures of the world were ephemeral and provided no lasting satisfaction.

"Is that all there is?" he might very well ask.

Even worse than his life on earth, however, is his future, for he will be separated from God—the source of all blessing and true happiness. That means God will deprive him of everything that gives quality or worthwhileness to existence. That is why regeneration, or the new birth, is very important. The Lord Jesus

Christ stressed the importance of the new birth when he said that one could never see or enter the kingdom of God unless he was born again (John 3:3, 5).

All of us should think seriously about these words of Christ: "Marvel not that I said unto thee, Ye must be born again." The new birth is not something to marvel about. While it is a supernatural work of the Spirit, it is indispensable to seeing and entering God's spirit kingdom. The sinful fall of Adam and Eve in the Garden of Eden made it absolutely necessary for one to be born again to be a fit subject for heaven.

COUNTERFEITS OF REGENERATION

No Biblical Warrant

Charles Spurgeon once said that a preacher should not tell his congregation what his subject was not, but get to the point and tell them what it was. While I do not disagree with that great preacher, I feel that the existence of so many counterfeits of regeneration make it necessary to be warned about them. So I am going to use this portion of the chapter to show you some of the counterfeits of regeneration.

Regeneration is not attending church. A local Bible-believing church is a good place to attend, even though some stay away because of their thread-bare excuse that the church is full of hypocrites. Many of the best people in society attend church and do many good things, but church attendance is not regeneration. One cannot be born again by attending church.

Regeneration is not church membership. Thousands become members of local churches, but that doesn't mean all of them are born again. One cannot be born again by joining a local church.

Regeneration is not baptism. Some churches teach that one is born again by being baptized. The false teaching of baptismal regeneration for adults and infants has deceived millions of people ever since it was introduced in the third century and came to be practiced more fully in and beyond the sixth century.

Regeneration is not reformation. People speak loosely about being born again. The man who stops being a drunk, a gambler, a cigarette smoker, a drug user, or an adulterer might say, "I've been born again!" But that cannot be, because to be born again is not turning over a new leaf by giving up bad habits. Some who have reformed their lives have gone so far as to say, "I am born again and on my way to heaven." But such is not true because regeneration is not reformation.

Regeneration is not conversion. Many Christians believe that the new birth, conversion, justification and salvation all mean the same thing. But they don't. Conversion is made up of repentance and faith. Some believe and many modern evangelists teach that one can be born again by the exercise of repentance and faith. But they have no biblical warrant for that idea.

Errors about Receiving the New Birth

I once believed conversion and regeneration were the same thing and preached that way as hundreds of preachers do today. It took me years to come to the correct relationship between regeneration and conversion.

Most modern evangelists preach a false doctrine of the new birth. They say one can effect his own new birth by going forward in a meeting and making a decision to let Jesus into his heart. Some of them say a man is born again by repenting and believing. But these are false evangelistic appeals, because nowhere in the New Testament will you find them used by Christ or his apostles. The unconverted is spiritually dead. Therefore he has no desire, ability, or will to exercise the spiritual functions of repentance and faith.

THE CHARACTER OF REGENERATION

Conversion Is Caused by the New Birth

The Bible says that repentance and faith are gifts of God. Since it is impossible for the natural man to receive the things of the Spirit of God (1 Corinthians 2:14), divine quickening must precede one's human response of repentance and faith.

The Bible says that "as many as were ordained to eternal life believed" (Acts 13:48). And Jesus said "that no man can come unto me, except it were given unto him of my Father" (John 6:65). Salvation from start to finish is the work of God as can be seen in these words of Paul: "Moreover whom he did predestinate, them he also called: and whom he called, them he also justified: and whom he justified, them he also glorified" (Romans 8:30). To be called of God includes being born again.

Conversion (made up of repentance and faith) is caused by regeneration which, in turn, is related to God's call and eternal purpose. Charles H, Spurgeon, who saw thousands come into the kingdom of God through his preaching and writing, said, "If any man is saved, it is not because he willed to be saved. If any man is brought to Christ, it is not of any effort of his, but the root, the cause, the motive of salvation of any one human being, and of all the chosen in heaven, is to be found in the predestinating purpose and sovereign distinguishing will of the Lord our God . . . Regeneration is an instantaneous work. Conversion to God, the fruit of regeneration, occupies all our life, but regeneration itself is effected in an instant."

Theologian A. A. Hodge put it this way: "Regeneration is God's act; conversion is ours. Regeneration is the implantation of a gracious principle; conversion is the exercise of that principle. Regeneration is never a matter of direct consciousness to the subject of it, conversion always is such to the agent of it. Regeneration is a single act, complete in itself and never repeated; conversion, as the beginning of holy living, is the commencement of a series constant, endless and progressive."

The Divine Power of Drawing

The unregenerate sinner is so depraved that with an un-changed heart and mind, he will never come to Christ. The change that is essential is one that God alone can effect. It is therefore by the divine drawing that one comes to Christ. Jesus said, "No man can come to me, except the Father which hath sent me draw him" (John 6:44).

By "drawing," Jesus meant the regenerating power of the Holy Spirit that convicts the sinner of his guilt before God. It also convinces the sinner that he is lost and without hope, and that his own self-righteousness has no merit with God. The "drawing" is the Holy Spirit awakening within the sinner a sense of his great need to be saved from his sins. It is the power of the Holy Spirit overcoming the pride of the natural man, so he is ready to come to Christ as one who recognizes his spiritual poverty. The Holy Spirit creates within him a new desire, abil-ity, and will to repent or turn from his sins and exercise faith in Jesus Christ as his Lord and Saviour.

Synonyms for Regeneration

Regeneration has several synonyms in the Bible. John the apostle called it born of God, born again, born of the Spirit, and passing from death unto life. Paul spoke of it as alive from the dead, a new creature, a resurrection, putting on the new man, washing of re-generation, and renewing of the Holy Spirit. Peter described re-generation as a call out of darkness into God's marvelous light, and being made a partaker of the divine nature.

All these expressions say that this is the same truth viewed from different sides. They describe a great radical change of heart and nature. This change is so thorough and complete that it could bear no better name than regeneration.

The New Birth and Physical Birth

The new spiritual birth is similar in some ways to one's physical birth. A Christian's physical birth was not of his doing. Neither was his new birth because it was accomplished exclusively by the Spirit of God. The believer cannot remember his physical birth, and he was unconscious of his new birth taking place. His physical birth preceded all of his physical activity and his spiritual birth precedes all of his spiritual activity.

Other facts of the new birth are not similar to physical birth. The physical birth is an observable event, but the new birth is mysterious because it cannot be observed. A physical birth does not always take place at a time planned by the parents, but the new birth is a sovereign act which takes place when and where and on whom God wills.

Many physical births are stillborn, but the new birth is always successful because everyone born again receives immortality or eternal life. Physical birth cannot produce spiritual abilities in the newborn, but everyone who is born again has spiritual abilities. These enable him to repent or turn from his sins, believe in Jesus Christ as his Lord and Saviour, and receive the power of the Holy Spirit, which enables him to love the Lord Jesus and to daily strive to live in "holiness without which no man shall see the Lord" (Hebrews 12:14).

Known Only by Its Effects

The impartation of a new nature is one that can only be known and discerned by its effects. This change is one that no man can give to himself. Nor can one do anything to cause the new birth of another. It is an internal and exclusive work of God with which man has nothing to do.

A boy with a marigold flower in his hand asked his father why it died when he pulled off its petals, but went on blooming if he left them on. "Because," said the wise father, "God works from the inside."

THE MEANS OF REGENERATION

The Folly of Baptismal Regeneration

Many believe that Jesus was speaking of literal water and baptismal regeneration when he said, "Except a man be born of water and of the Spirit, he cannot enter into the kingdom of God" (John 3:5). But that kind of teaching is false because it says in effect that no one was saved before John the Baptist, for the Old Testament does not mention baptism. It says that every professing believer who has died without baptism is lost. It would mean that some very godly people among the Quakers and in the Salvation Army would not be born again because they do not baptize.

It would mean we would have to ignore as wrong every passage in Scripture that teaches salvation is by grace and not of works. To teach baptismal regeneration is the same as saying Jesus was lying when he told the thief on the cross, who was not baptized, that he was going to be with him in paradise.

Though Christ commanded believers to be baptized, he did not say that it was the cause of regeneration. In fact, baptism is a profession of one's grace-and-faith identification with Christ's death, burial, and resurrection. That is why believer's baptism by immersion is the only mode of baptism that is in keeping with what the Bible teaches about it. For example, Paul the apostle made this identification when he wrote,

> Therefore we are buried with him by baptism into death: that like as Christ was raised up from the dead by the glory of the Father, even so we also should walk in newness of life. For if we have been planted together in the likeness of his death, we shall be also in the likeness of his resurrection.
>
> (Romans 6:4–5)

What Christ Meant by "Water"

If Christ did not mean literal water in John 3:5 what did he mean? We can find help in answering that question from the words of Christ to the woman at the well. After telling her that whoever drank the well water would get thirsty again, he said, "But whosoever drinketh of the water that I shall give him shall never thirst; but the water that I shall give him shall be in him a well of water springing up into everlasting life" (John 4:13–14). We can safely assume that he was not speaking of literal water.

Nor did he mean literal water when he said, "If any man thirst, let him come unto me and drink. He that believeth on me, as the scripture hath said, out of his belly shall flow rivers of living water" (John 7:37–38).

By comparing Scripture with Scripture it can be seen that the word "water" in John 3:5 means the Word of God. James and Peter believed that the new birth was an act of God's will using his Word. "Of his own will begat he us with the word of truth," said James, "that we should be a kind of firstfruits of his creatures" (James 1:18). And Peter said, "Being born again, not of corruptible seed, but of incorruptible, by the word of God, which liveth and abideth for ever" (1 Peter 1:23).

This does not mean that one can be born again by reading the Bible or by hearing a sermon that expounds a portion of Scripture. One's new birth is an exclusive work of the Spirit after which he learns from the Word how to repent, believe and live for Christ.

The Communication of Something New

Jesus said that the author of the new birth is the Holy Spirit and that human nature could do nothing to effect one's own new birth. "It is the Spirit," he said, that quickeneth; the flesh profiteth nothing: the words that I speak unto you, they are spirit, and they are life" (John 6:63). He also said that one could no more effect his own new birth than he could give direction to the wind (John 3:8).

The new birth is not the removal of anything from the sinner, nor the changing of anything within the sinner. It is rather the communication of something new to the sinner. The new birth is the implantation of a new life principle or new spiritual nature. When physically born, we received the nature of our parents. But when spiritually born, we become partakers of God's nature. Speaking of the precious promises of God, Peter said "that by these ye might be partakers of the divine nature, having escaped the corruption that is in the world through lust" (2 Peter 1:4).

The character of the new birth, then, is neither the reformation of the outward man, nor the education of the natural man, nor the purification of the old man. It is a divine begetting or the creation by God of a new man.

The word "spirit" comes from a Greek word meaning "wind," and Jesus likens the process of the new birth by the Spirit to the wind. It is an excellent illustration because the wind is irresistible, irregular, inscrutable, indispensable, invigorating, and invisible. We can see the rain, the snow, and the lightning, but we cannot see the wind.

THE NECESSITY FOR REGENERATION

The Natural Decline of Human Nature

The exceeding sinfulness that corrupts man's nature is the reason that regeneration is necessary if one is to receive and know the spiritual truths of God. Paul explained this when he wrote, "But the natural man receiveth not the things of the Spirit of God: for they are foolishness unto him: neither can he know them, because they are spiritually discerned" (1 Corinthians 2:14).

Just as rivers flow downward, sparks fly upward, and articles heavier than air fall to the ground, man's heart naturally leans toward that which is evil. He not only commits sin, but he loves sin. Every human being needs to be cleansed from sin's guilt, but he also needs to be delivered from sin's power. Paul describes this condition with the two words, "under sin" (Romans 3:9; Galatians

3:22). "Under sin" means more than being "guilty of sin" or "in bondage to sin." It is a general state likened to convicts under sentence in prison or a disease-stricken people under quarantine. Another strong description of the natural man is this one by Paul: "For God hath concluded them [Jew and Gentile] in unbelief" (Romans 11:32). That means they are shut up to unbelief!

Not Ready for Heaven

There are two distinct things that God does for every sinner he saves by his grace. First, he sends his Holy Spirit to regenerate the sinner, which makes him a new man. Second, he justifies him by legally declaring him righteous in his sight. This is possible because of this amazing transaction: He imputes Christ's righteousness to the believing sinner and imputes the sinner's guilt to Christ.

These two things are absolutely necessary for salvation. Without the change wrought by the new birth, one would have no desire or ability or will to repent and believe in Christ. Without justification one has no right or title to heaven. These are essential stages in God's *ordo salutis*—the order in which the Spirit applies redemption to those whom God chose before the foundation of the world. The stages of that order are as follows:

- The effectual call and new birth by the Spirit of God, which makes one a citizen of God's spirit kingdom and a member of his royal family.
- Conversion, which is made up of the gifts of repentance and faith.
- Justification, by which God legally declares the believing sinner to be righteous in his sight.
- Adoption, which gives the believer sonship privileges in the family of God.
- Sanctification, by which the Holy Spirit—who indwells the believer—sets him aside for God's holy use and assists him to progress in holiness of life.
- Glorification, which is the divine guarantee and certainty of a home in heaven after physical death.

Surely it is evident that the vast majority of people in the world see nothing, feel nothing, and know nothing about biblical Christianity as they ought. All the people in the world were born spiritually dead and are going to die physically. Everyone will be judged by God. Those who have been born again are now on the way that leads to eternal life in heaven, but those who are not born again, and go through life rejecting the offer of the gospel, are on the broad way that, as Christ said, leads to destruction! All the evidence points to the awful truth that most people are not prepared for heaven. In fact, they wouldn't be happy in heaven if they could get there. This chapter is entitled, "Why is Regeneration so Important" because there is no salvation, no spiritual life, and no heaven without regeneration.

THE MARKS OF REGENERATION

John the apostle records Christ's explanation of the new birth in his conversation with Nicodemus. He also describes the marks or proofs that a person has been born again.

- A regenerate man does not commit sin as a habit. Sin no longer pleases him. Though he may sin, he does not sin habitually or characteristically. That is what John meant when he said, "Whosoever is born of God doth not commit sin" (1 John 3:9).
- A regenerate man believes that Jesus Christ is the only Saviour by whom one may be justified and pardoned. "Whosoever believeth that Jesus is the Christ is born of God" (1 John 5:1).
- The regenerate man is a holy man. John said, "If ye know that he is righteous, ye know that every one that doeth righteousness is born of him" (1 John 2:29).
- A regenerate man has a special love for fellow saints. "We know that we have passed from death unto life," said John, "because we love the brethren" (1 John 3:14).

- A regenerate man does not make the world's opinion his rule of right and wrong. He does not mind going against the stream of the world's ways, notions, and customs. John put it this way: "For whatsoever is born of God overcometh the world: and this is the victory that overcometh the world, even our faith" (1 John 5:4).

- A regenerate man is careful of his soul. John said that "he that is begotten of God keepeth himself and that wicked one toucheth him not" (1 John 5:18).

A good example of one who manifested the marks of regeneration was George Whitefield of England, whom God used as the instrument in the eighteenth century American revival known as the "Great Awakening." One day someone asked him, "Why do you preach so often on 'Ye Must Be Born Again?'"

"Because," said Whitefield, "ye must be born again."

A right translation of "born again" is "born from above." This rendering shows why preachers and evangelists are wrong to tell people they can be born again by doing something such as going forward to decide for Christ, or repenting or believing or committing one's life to Christ. Regeneration means to be born from above. It is a supernatural act from heaven, and we should not be deceived by those who preach a man-centered gospel. And that is why regeneration is life's greatest truth.

CHAPTER TWELVE

IS A RESURRECTION INCREDIBLE?

Why should it be thought a thing incredible with you, that God should raise the dead?

(Acts 26:8)

The most searching question since the Garden of Eden is found in the first of the poetical or wisdom group of Old Testament books—the book of Job. "If a man die," asked Job, "shall he live again?" (Job 14:14). This is a question that thinking men of every generation have asked repeatedly, and for which multitudes have sought a satisfactory answer.

Men Are Not Animals

The late Andrew Carnegie, a steel magnate from Pittsburgh, Pennsylvania, offered to give anyone a million dollars if he could prove and convince him that there was life after death. The fact that men should seriously consider such a question is significant.

If there is no hereafter for the human race, for example, why would men, even for a moment, ask about the possibility of life after death? It is because men were made in the image of God, and they are not animals who have no spirit and do not live after death.

Spirit or Body?

Some years ago, the editor of a periodical called "The Outlook," published in New York City, gave a lecture before the Sunday Evening Club of Chicago. "The resurrection of Jesus Christ," he said in effect, "was not an extraordinary event. The resurrection of Jesus Christ was only an extraordinary manifestation of an ordinary event. Whenever a man dies, his spirit ascends to God, his Maker, and that is a resurrection. Death and resurrection spell the same thing."

That is erroneous teaching, for it makes the resurrection refer to the spirit of man and not to his body. It is the body that dies and is buried, and not the soul or spirit; and therefore it is the body that is raised from the dead, and not the soul or spirit.

Whenever the word resurrection is used in the Bible (and the word is found only in the New Testament), it refers to the body alone, and means that man's body of flesh and bones will be raised from the grave, and in that body he will meet God. This does not mean that the exact particles of the mortal body will be found in the resurrection body, but it means that the resurrection body will be identical with the body that is destroyed by death.

Ongoing Changes

Man's natural body is constantly undergoing changes. Waste matter is thrown off continually and replaced by new cells and material, and yet everyone recognizes that a man 70 years old has the same body as he had when he was 17 years old, although the actual substances composing it are entirely different. So the resurrection body will be a material, immortal body, identical with the mortal body, and revealing the same personality.

This teaching may seem incredible to some, but there is nothing too hard for God. In the words of the apostle Paul as he stood before King Agrippa, "Why should it be thought a thing incredible with you, that God should raise the dead?" (Acts 26:8).

IS A RESURRECTION POSSIBLE?

Everything God Does Is Wonderful

Christ, who created the worlds out of nothing (John 1:3) by the word of his power, is surely able to fashion a resurrection body out of something. This may seem wonderful or incredible to those who have never seen or handled a resurrection body, and it is. But as Charles Spurgeon, the noted London preacher, used to say: "Everything that God does is wonderful, until we get used to it."

When man becomes accustomed to God's wonders of creation, he ascribes those wonders to "Mother Nature" and forgets that they were created by God.

Paul at Mars Hill

The subject of the resurrection of the body of man has been disputed down through the centuries, ever since man began to die because of sin. When the apostle Paul spoke at Athens, on Mars Hill, for example, he closed his sermon with these words from Acts 17:30–32:

> But now God commandeth all men every where to repent: because he hath appointed a day, in which he will judge the world in righteousness by that man whom he hath ordained; whereof he hath given assurance unto all men, in that he hath raised him from the dead.

> And when they heard of the resurrection of the dead, some mocked: and others said, "We will hear thee again of this matter."
>
> (Acts 17:30–32)

Christ and the Sadducees

In the days of Christ and the apostles, some who did not believe in the resurrection of the dead were called Sadducees. They were religious and held the high priest and other ruling offices of the Jews, but they were unbelievers and opposed the truth. Here is the record of their conversation with Jesus in Matthew 22:23–33:

They said, "Master, Moses said, 'If a man die, having no children, his brother shall marry his wife, and raise up seed unto his brother.' Now there were with us seven brethren: and the first, when he had married a wife, deceased, and, having no issue, left his wife unto his brother: Likewise the second also, and the third, unto the seventh. And last of all the woman died also, Therefore in the resurrection whose wife shall she be of the seven? for they all had her."

"Ye do err," said Jesus, "not knowing the scriptures, nor the power of God. For in the resurrection they neither marry, nor are given in marriage, but are as the angels of God in heaven."

Then knowing their erroneous position on the resurrection, Jesus continued, "But as touching the resurrection of the dead, have ye not read that which was spoken unto you by God, saying, 'I am the God of Abraham, and the God of Isaac, and the God of Jacob?' God is not the God of the dead, but of the living."

Those who had heard this dialogue between Christ and the Sadducees were astonished at the teaching of Christ.

Here it is evident that Christ based his belief in the resurrection of the body on the tense of a verb. He called attention to the fact that God did not say (and it was God talking) "I was the God of Abraham" as though Abraham was not living; nor did he say "I was the God of Isaac, and the God of Jacob" as though they were no longer in existence; but he said "I *am* the God of Abraham, and the God of Isaac and the God of Jacob" showing they were alive at that time hundreds of years after they had died and would continue to live forever.

In the parallel passage in the gospel of Luke, Christ referred to Abraham, Isaac, and Jacob by saying, "Neither can they die anymore: for they are equal unto the angels; and are the children of God, being the children of the resurrection" (Luke 20:36).

The Apostles and the Pharisees

The Lord's answer silenced the Sadducees for a time, but unbelief is a very strong and persistent attitude. Consequently, the apostles found the same opposition from them when they were speaking to the people at the temple, right after Peter healed the man who was lame from birth.

> And as they spake unto the people, the priests, and the captain of the temple, and the Sadducees, came upon them, being grieved that they taught the people, and preached through Jesus the resurrection from the dead. And they laid hands on them, and put them in hold unto the next day: for it was now eventide.
>
> (Acts 4:1–3)

Paul and the Resurrection

The resurrection also was constantly preached by Paul, and that is one of the reasons he suffered so much, and spent many days in prison. Called before the Sanhedrin council and seeing that both Sadducees and Pharisees were there, he cried out, "Men and brethren, I am a Pharisee, the son of a Pharisee: of the hope and resurrection of the dead I am called in question" (Acts 23:6).

His words caused a dissension between the Pharisees and the Sadducees, and a division among the people, because the Sadducees taught that there was neither resurrection, nor angels, nor spirits, but the Pharisees believed and taught all three.

Later, when Paul stood before the Roman governor Felix in Caesarea, and after the Jewish leaders had made false accusations about him, he said, "And I have hope toward God, which they themselves also allow, that there shall be a resurrection of the dead, both of the just and the unjust . . . . Except it be for this one voice, that I cried standing among them, Touching the resurrection of the dead I am called in question by you this day" (Acts 24:15, 21).

The Sadducees Are Still with Us

Opposition to the resurrection has been constant throughout the history of Christianity, and it is the same today. The preaching of the Word of God that the bodies of all men "both the just and the unjust" will be raised from the dead, meets with bitter opposition.

The Sadducees are still with us under different names, and they vigorously deny the resurrection of the bodies of the dead. In fact they put on a religious facade, but like the Sadducees of the first century, they deny the resurrection and the existence of God's spiritual kingdom.

Unbelief in Resurrection Motivates Wickedness

One of the major reasons there is so much unbridled sin and crime is man's refusal to believe in a resurrection and a judgment. Someone has rightly said, "There is nothing so conducive to immorality as a disbelief in immortality."

Let people believe that there is no life beyond the grave, no resurrection of the body, no meeting of a righteous God in judgment, and no eternal punishment for man or devil, and they throw off all restraints. They give themselves over to the passions of the flesh and mind, and regard not the rights of their fellow men. As a result crime is on the increase, more convicts occupy our prisons, and acts of lawlessness are to be seen everywhere.

Whether men believe it or not, however, there is going to be a resurrection of the dead when "God shall bring every work into judgment, with every secret thing, whether it be good, or whether it be evil" (Ecclesiastes 12:14).

THE RESURRECTION OF THE RIGHTEOUS DEAD

Differences of Opinion

While the Scriptures teach the resurrection of all men, there is a difference of opinion among theologians as to whether all men will be raised at the same time. Some men and some creeds have advocated a general resurrection and a general judgment. The language of the New Testament, especially the words of the Lord Jesus Christ with emphasis on the resurrection of the just, seem to indicate that there will be two resurrections and at the same time.

Jesus spoke of "the resurrection of the just" (Luke 14:14). He also said that "all that are in the graves shall hear his voice, And shall come forth; they that have done good, unto the resurrection of life; and they that have done evil, unto the resurrection of damnation" (John 5:28–29). He also said four times that he would raise up believers in the last day (John 6:39, 40, 44, 54).

The Bible speaks of a resurrection of the just and the unjust, a resurrection of the righteous dead, and the wicked dead, a resurrection of life and one of damnation. No matter what opinion we have about the controversial verses of Revelation 20:5–6, the Holy Spirit inspired the apostle John to write in both verses that there is a first resurrection. This indicates a second resurrection.

When we talk about the righteous dead, we of course do not mean those who did anything in themselves to become righteous. We are describing those who repent of their sins, receive Christ as their Saviour, and receive the imputed righteousness of the Son of God.

An evangelical writer has well said, "The resurrection body is as literal as broiled fish," basing his statement on John 21:13 when the Lord Jesus ate fish and bread with his apostles at the Sea of Galilee after his resurrection.

THE RESURRECTION OF THE WICKED DEAD

Be Sure Your Sin Will Find You Out

Divine revelation concerning the wicked dead is quite meager. God has not seen fit to give very many details about those who reject his beloved Son, the Lord Jesus Christ. We do know that the wicked dead, includes not only the outrageous sinners, those who are licentious, ungodly, and lawless, but those who are the respectable, indifferent, and religious rejecters of truth about God's Son. "The wicked, through the pride of his countenance," said David, "will not seek after God: God is not in all his thoughts" (Psalm 10:4).

Speaking to the Israelites, Moses said, "Ye have sinned against the LORD; and be sure your sin will find you out" (Numbers 32:23). A man's sin will either find him out in his own body, the bodies of his children, or in his resurrection body. The law of the harvest never fails. "Be not deceived," said Paul; "God is not mocked: for whatsoever a man soweth, that shall he also reap. For he that soweth to his flesh shall of the flesh reap corruption; but he that soweth to the Spirit shall of the Spirit reap life everlasting" (Galatians 6:7, 8).

A Body of Abhorrence

The body of the wicked that goes to the lake of fire cannot be the body that the physical wicked have now but a resurrection body of abhorrence. Perhaps this is what Isaiah is describing in the last verse of the last chapter of his prophecy: "And they shall go forth, and look upon the carcasses of the men that have transgressed against me; for their worm shall not die, neither shall their fire be quenched; and they shall be an abhorrence unto all flesh."

Daniel also mentions the resurrection of the ungodly, "And many of those who sleep in the dust of the earth shall awake, some to everlasting life, and some to shame and everlasting contempt" (Daniel 12:2).

A New Day Has Struck

Is it possible that this book has fallen into the hands of an unbeliever who, after reading all this information about resurrection, might be asking, "What does all this have to do with me?" It should make you think and consider your situation. Unless you become right with God, your resurrection will be the resurrection of the wicked. But there is good news for you. A new day has struck. What is this new day?

Paul described it when he said, "God now commandeth all men everywhere to repent: Because he hath appointed a day, in the which he will judge the world in righteousness by that man whom he hath ordained; whereof he hath given assurance unto all men, in that he hath raised him from the dead" (Acts 17:30–31).

A Brilliant Condensation

In those few sentences, Paul the apostle gave a brilliant condensation of the Christian religion. The operative word in his statement was the word "repent." When Paul told those highly-intellectual Greek philosophers that they were to repent, he was following his Lord's example.

Speaking to unbelievers, Jesus said, "Except ye repent, ye shall all likewise perish" (Luke 13:3, 5).

The central truth of what Paul said to the Greek philosophers was this: God had appointed a day in which he would judge the world in righteousness. But why should those leading thinkers of their day believe that he was telling the truth? Paul provided the answer when he said that God had given assurance to all men by raising his only begotten Son from the dead. Christ's resurrection was God's guarantee that all men will be raised to be judged by Christ.

Questions for Self-Examination

And that is why every man should examine himself and ask these questions: "Have I truly repented and striven to turn from my sins? Have I genuinely changed my mind to see God as holy and myself as sinful? Have I rejected the false concepts of the world? Have I given up the false religious ideas I may have been taught? And have I separated myself from the wicked lifestyle of the current, ungodly culture?

Every one of us must make sure that he is right with God. Since God has commanded all men everywhere to repent, we must be certain that we know what it means to repent and that we have sincerely repented—that is, turned from sin and turned to God through faith in Jesus Christ.

Reactions to Paul's Message

Some mocked at Paul's reference to the resurrection of Christ. Others procrastinated and said, "We will hear you again of this matter." When did they begin to mock and procrastinate? At the point of resurrection? No, that was just their excuse. They mocked and procrastinated at the point of moral application when Paul said that God commanded them to repent.

They did not believe in a resurrection, and that was one of their philosophical ideas. It is amazing how often men will employ an intellectual excuse for refusing to make a moral decision when God commands them to do so. Human nature is the same today as it was in the days of Paul. When Paul heard their opposition to the truth of resurrection and judgment, he left the meeting.

When men were angry with Paul, he often argued with them and triumphed over them. When men persecuted him, he courageously went back to the places where he had been persecuted. But for those who used intellectual flippancy and moral dishonesty, Paul had no further word. Jesus often did the same when confronted with hypocritical Pharisees.

But mocking and procrastinating were not the final results or reactions to Paul's message. Some of the people who had heard him ran after Paul, put their arms around him and told him they believed what he had said. It is significant that God's Word did not name any of those who rejected the truth, but it does name the ones who believed. Their names were, "Dionysius the Areopagite, and a woman named Damaris, and others with them" (Acts 17:34).

Jefferson's Bible

Here's a story to further the doctrine of resurrection and to show how men have introduced errors and denials of its truth. When my youngest son, Daniel, was graduating from elementary school and ready to go into junior high school, the school system offered a trip to Virginia and the nation's capital at Washington D.C. My wife and I thought it would be an excellent opportunity for Danny, not only to see, but to learn some very important historical facts about our country. We scraped together the money he needed and sent him off by bus from West Virginia.

On the trip home, the bus stopped at Monticello, the former home of Thomas Jefferson, the third President of the United States. Danny, who was very grateful for the trip that his mother and I had given him, took the rest of the little money he had with him and bought me a *Jefferson Bible*. Knowing that I was a Baptist minister, he was sure that I would appreciate the gift.

Thomas Jefferson was not only the third President of the United States. He was also a brilliant statesman who was the author of the famous Declaration of Independence. When he died on July 4th, 1826 (the 50th anniversary of the signing of the Declaration of Independence), his last words were, "I resign my spirit to God, my daughter to my country."

Although the Declaration of Independence uses such phrases as "Supreme Judge of the World," protection of "Divine Providence," and the words "God" and "Creator," it does not contain the name of Jesus Christ. The reason is that Thomas Jefferson was a deist, not a Christian. Deism is "a belief in the existence of a supreme being arising from reason rather than revelation." Unknown to many people, Jefferson did not believe that Jesus Christ was God, and he did not believe in the resurrection of Jesus Christ.

The *Jefferson Bible* deletes the deity of Jesus Christ, and even ends with Christ's body in the tomb of Joseph of Arimathaea. I had to take my 12-year-old son aside and very carefully explain to him why the *Jefferson Bible* was a very dangerous, deceitful, untrue book denying the resurrection of the Lord Jesus Christ.

I find it very difficult along with many others and also very sad to think that a man with Thomas Jefferson's brilliant mind would reject the evidence for the resurrection of Jesus Christ. The Devil has tripped up thousands because of their education and rationalization.

Belief in Resurrection Essential to Salvation

The apostles preached the resurrection of Christ wherever they went in the Roman Empire. They made it transparently clear that to disbelieve this great truth of God's Word was to suffer eternal separation from God, the source of all blessing. In Romans 10:9–10 Paul wrote,

> If thou shalt confess with thy mouth the Lord Jesus, and shalt believe in thine heart that God hath raised him from the dead, thou shalt be saved. For with the heart man believeth unto righteousness; and with the mouth confession is made unto salvation.

Notice that Paul used the word "heart" as that in which one must believe in the resurrection. The "heart" speaks of the affection, so one must sincerely desire to believe that God raised Christ from the dead. The resurrection of Jesus Christ is not only credible, but belief in that truth is absolutely necessary for one to be saved. One cannot honestly profess to be a Christian who does not believe in the resurrection of Christ.

Using the educational device of reverse implication, here is what Paul is saying in Romans 10:9: "If you will not confess with your mouth the Lord Jesus, and will not believe in your heart that God has raised him from the dead, you shall not be saved."

First Begotten of the Dead

The last book in the Bible pays homage to the Lord Christ and his glorious resurrection. Appearing to John the apostle, who feared the sight so much he fell at his feet as dead, Jesus laid his right hand on him and said, "Fear not; I am the first and the last: I am he that liveth, and was dead; and, behold I am alive for evermore, Amen; and have the keys of hell and of death" (Revelation 1:18).

John himself said that the book of Revelation was from "Jesus Christ, who is the faithful witness, and the first begotten of the dead, and the prince of the kings of the earth. Unto him that loved us and washed us from our sins in his own blood, and hath made us kings and priests unto God and his Father; to him be glory and dominion for ever and ever. Amen" (Revelation 1:5–6).

God's Personal Guarantee

What great blessings there are in the doctrine of resurrection! Death has no sting for believers, and the grave has no victory over them. They belong to Christ, who took part of human flesh and blood "that through death he might destroy him that had the power of death, that is the devil; and deliver them who through fear of death were all their lifetime subject to bondage" (Hebrews 2:14–15).

The resurrection of our Saviour, the Lord Jesus Christ is God's personal guarantee of our resurrection. In the light of his infallibly proved resurrection, no one should think it incredible that God has the power to raise the dead. The biblical truth about the subject of resurrection by the almighty power of God is such a wonderful doctrine, it should move us to sing these lines with hymn writer Christopher Wordsworth:

Hallelujah! Hallelujah!
Hearts to heaven and voices raise;
Sing to God a hymn of gladness,
Sing to God a hymn of praise;
He, who on the cross a victim,
To redeem his people, bled;
Jesus Christ, the King of glory,
Now is risen from the dead.

Christ is risen, we are risen;

Shed upon us heavenly grace,
Rain, and dew, and gleams of glory,
From the brightness of thy face;
So that we, with hearts in heaven,
Here on earth may fruitful be,
And by angel hands be gathered,
And be ever Lord with thee.

May our gracious God give you the wisdom to believe and rest in these words of the Lord Jesus from John 11:25–26: "I am the resurrection and the life: he that believeth in me, though he were dead, yet shall he live: and whosoever liveth and believeth in me shall never die. Believest thou this?"

CHAPTER THIRTEEN

WHAT IS THE FRUIT OF JUSTIFICATION?

Moreover whom he did predestinate, them he also called: and whom he called, them he also justified: and whom he justified, them he also glorified.

(Romans 8:30)

A born-again sinner is justified the moment he exercises the gift of faith in Jesus Christ. To be justified is to be declared righteous in the sight of God. And it should not surprise us to know that the Bible links glorification with justification. That means that every sincere believer in Jesus Christ cannot finally come short of salvation. If one is justified he must, in due time, be glorified—that is, go to heaven to live with Christ forever. What a wonderful promise!

A *Fait Accompli*

Paul used "glorified" in the past tense as though it had already taken place, because what God has determined may be viewed as certain. There is absolutely nothing that can prevent one who is justified from being glorified. You might say "It is a *fait accompli*." The language construction of Romans 8:30—"called, justified, and glorified"—expresses the certainty of the counsel of God's own will.

This idea of things in the future being described as already having taken place can be found also in the Old Testament because the promises of God are infallible. More than 600 years before Christ was born, for example, the prophet predicted his birth by saying, "Unto us a child is born, unto us a son is given" (Isaiah 9:6).

Christ also spoke of what was future as already past when he said, "I have finished the work which thou gavest me to do . . . . Now I am no more in the world" (John 17:4, 11).

Paul used the past tense of "glorified" because it was in accordance with the object he had in view: to console believers amidst their afflictions. When we suffer in this life and all things appear to conspire for our ruin, the Word of God describes us as already glorified. It is as though during the combat we have already won.

Pleasures Forever More

In Romans 8, Paul presents the commencement, the progress, and the consummation of salvation. Its commencement was laid in the eternal purpose of God, and its consummation in the eternal glory of the elect. Those whom God has predestined the Holy Spirit calls to new spiritual life by way of the new birth, to repentance, and to faith in Christ. Having imputed the guilt of believers to Christ and Christ's righteousness to them, God was legally able to justify them. And he will glorify all those whom he has justified.

To be glorified is to be completely conformed to the image or likeness of Jesus Christ and to see him as he is, and to enjoy the happiness anticipated by David when he wrote, "Thou wilt show me the path of life: in thy presence is fullness of joy; at thy right hand there are pleasures for evermore" (Psalm 16:11).

Not Glorified at Death

Some say, "That sounds wonderful! Maybe death isn't so bad after all." Hold on: You are not glorified when you die! The glorification of the saints will take place in the day of the blessed resurrection when their bodies shall be made like unto Christ's glorious body.

The believer will be glorified when his natural body, which was sown in corruption, in dishonour, and in weakness, shall be raised a spiritual body in power, incorruption and glory. Then death will be swallowed up in victory, all tears shall be wiped away, the Lamb will lead and feed them, and God shall be all in all.

THE PROCESS OF GLORIFICATION

What Happens When I Die?

If believers are not finally glorified until the resurrection at the coming of Christ, some ask these questions: "What happens when I die?" "Where are the dead?" This subject has bothered people for centuries. Who does not want to know all he can about what takes place after death?

As we saw in chapter twelve, Andrew Carnegie went so far as to offer one million dollars to anyone who could prove to his satisfaction the reality of life beyond the grave.

Two Distinct Natures

The Bible proves conclusively that man has two distinct natures: physical and spiritual. Some believe that man's nature is threefold because Paul said, "I pray God your whole spirit, and soul, and body be preserved blameless unto the coming of our Lord Jesus Christ" (1 Thessalonians 5:2).

I am not going to discriminate between the soul and the spirit. Since the terms are used interchangeably in Scripture, I will use them to indicate the spiritual nature of man. Biblical proof of the two natures of man can be found in the following verses:

For ye are bought with a price: therefore glorify God in your body and in your spirit which are God's. (1 Corinthians 6:20)

For what man knoweth the things of a man, save the spirit of man which is in him? Even so the things of God knoweth no man, but the Spirit of God. (1 Corinthians 2:11)

Let us cleanse ourselves from all filthiness of the flesh and spirit perfecting holiness in the fear of God. (2 Corinthians 7:11)

Some years ago, the Associate Press published an article about Dr. William Mayo, a world famous surgeon, the senior of two equally famous Mayo brothers, and chief of staff at the Mayo Clinic in Rochester, Minnesota. "The keen blade of my scalpel," said Dr. Mayo, "may never uncover the soul as a tangible part of the mystery called man, but I know it is there. I am as confident of its presence as I am of the most elemental truth to which my own medical science adheres."

Death Separates Soul from Body

The Bible says, "There is no man that hath power over the spirit to retain the spirit; neither hath he power in the day of death" (Ecclesiastes 8:8). The same writer also said, "Then shall the dust return to the earth as it was and the spirit shall return to God who gave it" (12:7).

We often hear people say about the deceased, "He gave up the ghost." The Bible uses the same words regarding the deaths of Abraham, Isaac, Jacob, and Christ. Those words show that at death there is a separation of the spirit from the body.

When Elijah prayed in Zarephath for the dead son of a widow he said, "O Lord my God, I pray thee, let this child's soul come into him again. And the Lord heard the voice of Elijah and the soul of the child came into him again, and he revived" (1 Kings 17:21–22).

God's original decree of death is a clear separation of the spirit from the body. It consigns only the dust or the body to the earth, while the spirit returns to God who gave it.

The Doctrine of the Intermediate State

What happens to the spirits of those who die? Are they roaming out there in the vast darkness of space? Is there any difference between what happens to the spirits of believers and the spirits of unbelievers? The answers to these questions points us to the doctrine of the intermediate state.

In the earliest years of the church, there was little material on this doctrine. The belief that the Lord would soon return as judge made the interval seem to be of little consequence. The intermediate state became a problem when it became apparent that Christ would not return at once. All the early church fathers were not in agreement. The majority of them, however, sought to solve the mystery of what happens to the spirit after death by assuming a distinct, intermediate state between death and resurrection.

In his book, *Life Beyond Death*, Addison said, "For many centuries the general conclusion was widely accepted that in a subterranean Hades the righteous enjoyed a measure of reward not equal to their future heaven, and the wicked suffered a degree of punishment not equal to their future hell. The intermediate state was thus a slightly reduced version of ultimate retribution."

This view was held, though with some variations, by Justin Martyr, Ireneus, Tertullian, Novation, Origen, Gregory of Nyssa, Ambrose, and Augustine. In the Alexandrian School, the idea passed into that of gradual purification of the soul, and this, in the course of time, paved the way for the Roman Catholic doctrine of purgatory.

Gregory of Nazianze, Eusebius, and Gregory the Great favored the idea that at death the souls of the righteous immediately entered heaven. In the middle ages the doctrine of the intermediate state was retained, and in this connection the Roman Catholic Church developed the doctrine of purgatory.

The Reformers and the Creeds

The Protestant Reformers, however, rejected purgatory and threw out the idea of a real intermediate state. They believed that those who died in the Lord immediately entered the bliss of heaven, but those who died in their sins descended into hell.

In answer to the question, "What comfort does the resurrection of the body afford thee?" the Heidelberg Catechism says, "Not only my soul, after this life, shall be immediately taken up to Christ its Head, but also that this body, raised by the power of Christ, shall again be united with my soul, and made like the glorious body of Christ."

Writing about the same subject, those who wrote The Westminster Confession of Faith, said, "The souls of the righteous, being made perfect in holiness, are received into the highest heavens, where they behold the face of God in light and glory, waiting for the full redemption of their bodies."

The Hebrew Word *Sheol*

In the Old Testament, *sheol* is the Hebrew word used to designate the place of the souls of the dead. Actually, the word *sheol* is a neutral term, indicating neither happiness nor misery. In a broad sense, it often means "grave" or "death." Several Old Testament passages describe descent into *sheol* as punishment against the wicked (Psalm 9:17).

The word *sheol* is recorded 65 times in the Old Testament: In the King James Version it is translated 31 times as "hell," 31 times as "grave," and three times as "pit." The word *sheol*, however, does not mean hell, grave or pit. The Hebrew dictionary in *Strong's Exhaustive Concordance* says, "*Sheol* is the world of the dead." *Young's Analytical Concordance* says it is "the unseen state." And *Smith's Dictionary* says, *Sheol* is always the abode of the departed spirits. But in many instances we believe it was translated 'hell' because the reference is clearly to that part or compartment of *Sheol* where the wicked are punished.

Here is an interesting note: The word *sheol* is never used in the plural, for it is one place (abode of spirits). The Hebrew word for grave, however, is used many times in the plural, which seems to prove that there are many graves, but only one *sheol*. The Bible never says the body goes to *sheol*, and it never says the spirit goes to the grave.

The Greek Word *Hades*

The place of the souls of the dead is called *hades* in the New Testament, and, like *sheol* of the Old Testament, it is always used

194

in the same sense. *Hades* appears 11 times in the New Testament and is translated in the English Bible 10 times as "hell," and once as "the grave" (1 Corinthians 15:55). The dictionaries and concordances also say it is the place of departed spirits.

The Greek word from which the English word "hell" is translated is *gehenna,* which is found 11 times in the New Testament, ten of which were spoken by the Lord Jesus.

Two Compartments in *Hades*

Some students of the Bible believe there has been a change in *sheol* and *hades.* In 20 of the 65 Old Testament references to *sheol,* its location is described as downward. "I will go down to *Sheol.*" The same is true of *Hades* in the New Testament: "Thou shalt be brought down to Hades." The Old Testament sheds very little light on what kind of place *sheol* is. It says nothing about the spirits of the righteous and unrighteous. It makes no great distinction between them: They just depart to *sheol.*

Why is this? I think the answer is found in the New Testament, because the conditions beyond the grave were not revealed in the Old Testament. That revelation was reserved for our Lord Jesus Christ. Paul revealed the answer when he wrote that the saving grace "was given to us in Christ Jesus before the world began. But is now made manifest by the appearing of our Saviour Jesus Christ, who hath abolished death, and hath brought life and immortality to light through the gospel" (2 Timothy 1:9–10).

Christ came to save sinners, but this passage says he also came to bring life and immortality to light. Notice carefully that Paul did not say that Christ came to bring into existence, but into light. The Lord Jesus seemed to indicate in Luke 16:19–31 that there were two compartments in *hades:* Abraham's bosom, a place of comfort for the righteous; and a place of torment for the wicked.

Hades and Paradise

The Bible seems to imply that when Christ died he went to *hades.* He had told the dying thief, "Verily, I say unto thee, Today thou shalt be with me in paradise" (Luke 23:43). Paradise is another name for Abraham's bosom. It is my view that, since Christ's resurrection and ascension, *hades* is no longer below, but above. This seems to be what Paul implied when he said, "Wherefore he saith, When he ascended up on high, he led captivity captive, and gave gifts unto men. (Now that he ascended, what is it but that he also descended first into the lower parts of the earth? He that descended is the same also that ascended up far above all heavens, that he might fill [fulfill] all things)" (Ephesians 4:8–10).

Paradise is an oriental term that means "parks or pleasure gardens." It occurs only three times in the Bible: Luke 23:43; 2 Corinthians 12:4; and Revelation 2:7. Paradise is a form of heaven, the good part of *hades*. It is the place where Christ is at present— the place where he manifests his presence and glory. It is sometimes said that for the redeemed, paradise is heaven without the body, or that it is the place before the resurrection.

Is There an Intermediate Body?

Some Christians think that there is an intermediate body. They base their belief on Paul's words about "a building made of God, an house not made with hands, eternal in the heavens. For in this we groan, earnestly desiring to be clothed upon with our house which is from heaven: if so that being clothed we shall not be found naked" (2 Corinthians 5:1–3).

They also see an intermediate body in the account of Christ's transfiguration (Matthew 17:1–9). Those who say that the transfiguration was just a vision are contradicted by Luke 9, where Luke's account of the transfiguration scene is recorded.

Luke wrote that Peter and those with him were awake and saw two men talking with Christ, who were identified as Moses and Elijah. Luke also said that they saw Christ's glory and the two men who stood with him. It is obvious that Moses and Elijah appeared to the disciples in some form of bodies. Though some Christians think they were intermediate bodies, the Bible does not enlighten us as to what kind of bodies they were.

A Good Definition of Glorification

So far we have learned the following: The Bible teaches that final glorification will not take place until Christ's coming and our resurrection. The key verse that teaches this is 1 Corinthians 15:23. Glorification does not refer to the blessedness that the spirits of believers enter at death. The transformation of the people of God at death is glorious, and to depart and be with Christ is far better. But that is not their glorification. It is not the goal of the believer's hope and expectation.

The resurrection that Christ secured for his people is redemption, not only from sin, but from all its consequences. Death is the wages of sin, and the death of the believer does not deliver him the wages. The last enemy death has not been destroyed and has not yet been swallowed up in victory. Hence glorification has in view the destruction of death itself. Paul provided a good definition of glorification when he wrote, "And not only they, but ourselves also, which have the first fruits of the Spirit, even we ourselves groan within ourselves waiting for the redemption of our body" (Romans 8:23).

THE PERVERSIONS OF GLORIFICATION

The Doctrine of Purgatory

The Roman Catholic Church teaches that sin is forgiven in four ways. First, original sin is removed in the waters of baptism. Second, daily sins are removed by the so-called sacrifice of the mass in which the priest claims to have the power to change the bread and wine into the body and blood of Christ. Third, venial sins before God are removed by extreme unction (the last rites of the Church). And fourth, what sins are left over are removed by the fires of purgatory.

Romanism also teaches that those who die at peace with the church, but are not perfect, pass into purgatory. All adults who have not been baptized and those who, after their baptism, have committed mortal sin go immediately to hell. The Roman Catholic

Church also teaches that Catholics who die and go to purgatory make satisfaction for their sins committed after baptism by suffering a longer or shorter time according to their degree of guilt. It also teaches the false idea that the Church on earth has power by prayers and the sacrifice of the mass to shorten such sufferings or to remit them altogether.

All of this is in direct contrast to what the Bible teaches. A careful examination of the passages that speak of the intermediate state shows that believers do not suffer in an attempt to atone for their sins. Christ met all the preceptive and penal demands of the law on behalf of all believers. Furthermore, the Bible does not teach that the Church has the power to relieve sinners from the consequences of their sins either in this life or after death.

Only God can forgive sin and the church is authorized only to declare that fact to all who will repent from their sins and believe in Christ as their Lord and Saviour. The teaching of Romanism is false because it is inconsistent with the biblical teaching of the completeness and finality of Christ's satisfaction for the sins of his people, and with the doctrine of justification through faith alone.

In modern America, the Roman Catholic Church tries to hide from Protestants its teaching that souls in purgatory suffer from actual fire. Their writings, however, show that to be wrong.

Saint Thomas Aquinas, for example, taught that the pains of purgatory are as violent as hell.

Cardinal Bellarmine said, "It is the same sensible punishment which the sinner ought to have suffered in hell, with the exception of eternity."

The Sunday Visitor, the popular Catholic weekly, said, "Purgatory is real: it is a suburb of hell . . . the sense of pains of purgatory equal those of hell. Which means the temperature is about the same in both regions" (26 November 1945).

The Council of Trent declared, "If anyone saith that after the gift of justification has been received, to every penitent sinner the guilt is remitted and the debt of eternal punishment is blotted out in such a way that no debt of temporal punishment remains to be discharged either in this world or in the next in purgatory, before the entrance to the kingdom of heaven can be opened to him, let him be anathema."

A former priest, L. H. Lehmann, spoke of the sense of fear Catholics experience from purgatory and other doctrines of the Roman Catholic Church. "A sense of constant fear," he said, "overshadowed everything. Ingrained fear is, in fact, the predominant note running through the life of all children born and reared in Catholic Ireland. Few ever get rid of it completely in after [later] life, even in America. That fear concerns everything in this life on earth, and still more terrible is the fear of the terrors in the life beyond the grave" (*The Soul of a Priest*, p. 34).

The Doctrine of a Second Chance

Some teach that all who die in their sins will be given a second time of probation or a second chance to be saved. Opinions vary among Jehovah's Witnesses, Universalists, and some forms of Modernism as to whether a second chance is offered to all or only to certain classes. They believe that all who die in infancy and those who never heard the gospel in this life will receive the opportunity or a second chance to do so.

This idea is based on humanitarian conjectures or surmises of what God in his love and goodness might be expected to do. It is also developed from a desire to extend the efficacy of the atonement to as many as possible instead of establishing belief on a "Thus saith the Lord."

The Bible says that the state of the righteous and the wicked after death is fixed—it cannot be changed. Christ said that between them "there is a great gulf fixed" (Luke 16:26). Christ also described the state of the wicked as one of "outer darkness" where there will be "weeping and wailing and gnashing of teeth" (Matthew 8:12). And to the apostate Jewish Pharisees he said, "If ye believe not that I am he, ye shall die in your sins" (John 8:24).

One can sense the finality of the eternal condition after death in these words of Paul: "Behold now is the accepted time; behold now is the day of salvation" (2 Corinthians 6:2). There will be no "accepted time" or "day of salvation" after death! Not one verse of Scripture supports the idea of a second chance after death. This false doctrine is the result of denying the apostolic doctrine of the organic unity of the race in Adam's transgression in the Garden of Eden, and the biblical doctrine of eternal punishment.

The Doctrine of Soul Sleep

The various groups of Seventh Day Adventists believe in soul sleep—that the soul sleeps at death and continues that way until the resurrection. Most of those who believe in soul sleep do not believe in hell or a place of eternal punishment. Historically, however, the main body of Christians have opposed the idea of soul sleep. John Calvin, for example, wrote a paper against a certain sect of the Anabaptists who believe in soul sleep.

Death is not extinction but only separation of the soul from the body. The soul continues to exist fully conscious and active and at the resurrection, the same soul, not a new one, is reunited with the body. In the case of the wicked, it is ludicrous to say, as some do, that sinners should be brought back into existence for the sole purpose of putting them out of existence a second time.

When the Bible uses the word "sleep" to describe the death of the saints, it refers to the body, not the soul. In answer to the penitent thief on the cross, Jesus said, "Verily I say unto thee, Today thou shalt be with me in Paradise" (Luke 23:43). There is no suggestion here that the thief's soul would be going into a state of sleeping. When Jesus was transfigured with Moses and Elijah who had died years before, they were not sleeping, but active and engaged in conversation with Christ.

The Doctrine of Annihilation

Some cults believe that men and women found guilty after God judges them will be annihilated. Many hold to this theory in an attempt to defend the character of God. "We cannot believe," they say, "that a loving God would consign some of those he created to everlasting flames!" They also argue that the Bible uses "destroy, perish, and perdition more than it uses fire to describe the punishment of the wicked."

But those who disagree say that their idea is easily refuted by showing that the Greek word *aionios*, translated "eternal" and "everlasting" in the English Bible, was used by Christ to describe both the extent of the life of the righteous after death and the extent of the punishment of the wicked after death. "And these," said Christ, "shall go away into everlasting punishment: but the righteous into life eternal" (Matthew 25:46). "If the life of the righteous is everlasting," they say, "the punishment of the wicked must also be everlasting."

The doctrine of annihilation does violence to the biblical doctrine of divine justice. God's justice demands that the impenitent sinner be punished. Sin has wrought such a tremendous change in man that he cannot live in the presence of the unapproachable holiness of God unless he has been born again with a new spiritual life that enables him to live in God's spiritual kingdom. Even the angels who, under the leadership of Satan, sinned against God were not annihilated, but cast out of his presence to ultimately experience everlasting punishment.

Those who teach the doctrine of annihilation teach there will be no resurrection of the wicked. But the following passages of the Bible refute that idea:

John 5:28–29: "Marvel not at this," said Jesus, "for the hour is coming, in the which all that are in the graves shall hear his voice, and shall come forth; they that have done good, unto the resurrection of life; and they that have done evil, unto the resurrection of damnation."

Acts 24:15: Paul said that "there shall be a resurrection of the dead, both of the just and unjust."

Daniel 12:2: "And many of them that sleep in the dust of the earth shall awake, some to everlasting life, and some to shame and everlasting contempt."

The Doctrine of Spiritualism

Spiritualism is the belief that the spirits of the dead can and do communicate with the living usually through a medium who claims to be susceptible to their influences. The Bible teaches that it is impossible to communicate with the dead. In his story of the rich man and Lazarus, Jesus said it was impossible for Lazarus to go back to earth to warn the rich man's brothers.

The Word of God strictly forbids all attempts by the living to effect communication with the spirits of the dead. In the days of Israel, it was a capital crime. "For all that do these things," said Moses, "are an abomination unto the Lord" (Deuteronomy 18:12). That is why God declared that an attempt to communicate with the spirits of the dead was a sin deserving the death penalty.

God punished Saul, the first king of Israel, with death for consulting the witch of Endor in an attempt to communicate with the spirit of the dead Samuel. The Bible says that "Saul died for his transgression which he committed against the Lord, even against the word of the Lord, which he kept not, and also for asking counsel of one that had a familiar spirit, to enquire of it; and enquired not of the Lord: therefore he slew him, and turned the kingdom unto David the son of Jesse" (1 Chronicles 10:13–14). How true the words of the poet Rudyard Kipling:

Oh, the road to Endor is the oldest road,
And the craziest road of all.
Straight it runs to the witch's abode
As it did in the days of Saul.

And nothing has changed
Of the sorrow in store,
For such as go down
On the road to Endor

THE BENEFITS OF GLORIFICATION

The Saints Will Be Glorified Together

The truth that glorification must wait for the resurrection means that all the people of God will enter heaven together at the same point in time. There is no priority for some above others. Though death is an individual event, it is not so with glorification. None will have any advantage over others. All the saints will be glorified together with Christ. Paul the apostle emphasized this in 1 Corinthians 15 and in 1 Thessalonians 4.

The glorification of the elect will coincide with the final act of the Father in his exaltation and glorification of the Son. Paul said that the children of God are "heirs of God, and joint-heirs with Christ; if so be that we suffer with him, that we may be also glorified together" (Romans 8:17).

Glorification and Creation

The glorification of believers is bound up with the renewal of all creation. God will deliver not only believers from the bondage of corruption, but he will also deliver creation itself from that bondage. Here is how Paul explains that deliverance:

> For the creation was made subject to vanity, not willingly, but by reason of him who hath subjected the same in hope, because the creation itself also shall be delivered from the bondage of corruption into the glorious liberty of the children of God. For we know that the whole creation groaneth and travaileth in pain together until now. And not only they, but ourselves also, which have the firstfruits of the Spirit, even we ourselves groan within ourselves, waiting for the adoption, to wit, the redemption of our body.
>
> (Romans 8:20–23)

Glorification and Human Nature

Another benefit of the process of glorification is the believer's release from his sinful human nature. At the end of our pilgrim journey, whether at death or living when Christ returns, we will be delivered from our lifelong conflict with our sinful nature. Paul said that during our pilgrimage, our flesh lusts against our spirit and our spirit against the flesh. Then, contemplating the end of that conflict, he said, "Henceforth there is laid up for me a crown of righteousness, which the Lord, the righteous judge, shall give me at that day: and not to me only, but unto all them also that love his appearing" (2 Timothy 4:8).

Here we are citizens of the spiritual kingdom of God. At that time we will become inhabitants of that kingdom. Since we are citizens of God's kingdom, in this life we are ambassadors of Christ, strangers and pilgrims in a strange country. We can look forward, however, to going home to a country in which we have citizenship papers signed, as it were, by the shed blood of Jesus Christ.

Glorification Gives a Transformed Body

The greatest benefit of glorification will be a resurrection body like unto Christ's own body. "For our citizenship," said Paul, "is in heaven; from whence also we look for the Saviour, the Lord Jesus Christ: who shall change our vile body, that it may be fashioned like unto his glorious body, according to the working whereby he is able to subdue all things unto himself" (Philippians 3:20–21).

As one would expect, the infallible Word of God contains a central and exhaustive passage that bears upon this great theme of the resurrection of the believer's body. That passage is 1 Corinthians 15. Here are a few words from that passage in which Paul answers the questions, "How are the dead raised up? And with what body do they come?"

All flesh is not the same flesh: but there is one kind of flesh of men, another flesh of beasts, another of fishes, and another of birds. There are also celestial bodies, and bodies terrestrial: but the glory of the celestial is one, and the glory of the terrestrial is another. There is one glory of the sun, and another glory of the moon, and another glory of the stars: for one star differeth from another star in glory. So also is the resurrection of the dead. It is sown [or buried] in corruption; it is raised in incorruption: It is sown in dishonour; it is raised in glory: it is sown in weakness; it is raised in power: it is sown a natural body; it is raised a spiritual body. There is a natural body, and there is a spiritual body.

(1 Corinthians 15:39–44)

In this passage, Paul shows that there is a great variety of forms and bodies in God's creation. So we should not think it strange that God will give the resurrected or translated believer a transformed body. This aspect of truth is concluded with these assuring words by Paul: "And as we have borne the image of the earthy, we shall also bear the image of the heavenly" (1 Corinthians 15:49).

One of the Great Realities

If the believer's destiny were not clearly asserted in Scripture, it would be difficult for anyone to believe it. Look at the many false ideas that unbelievers have embraced about the afterlife. But the testimony of God's inerrant Word cannot be diminished or refuted by such foolish ideas. "Beloved now are we the sons of God," said John the apostle, "and it doth not yet appear what we shall be: but we know that when he shall appear, we shall be like him; for we shall see him as he is" (1 John 3:2).

The Lord works out his plan to redeem a people for himself right to the end that his sovereign, redemptive grace may be revealed. God's grace is infinite and therefore requires that the undertakings which measure his grace shall extend into infinite realms. Likewise, God wrought salvation to satisfy his infinite love, and, in the satisfying of his love, God does great things for his children—the objects of his affection. Conformity to the image of Christ is one of the great realities in the universe, and divine love can be content with nothing less as the measure of its achievement.

Glorification will be the answer to this prayer by our Saviour: "Father, I will that they also, whom thou hast given me, be with me where I am; that they may behold my glory, which thou hast given me: for thou lovedst me before the foundation of the world" (John 17:24).

"Now unto him that is able to keep you from falling, and to present you faultless before the presence of his glory with exceeding joy, to the only wise God our Saviour, be glory and majesty, dominion and power, both now and forever. Amen" (Jude 24–25).

SALVATION IS OF THE LORD!
Jonah 2:9

To order additional copies of

Searching Questions

Have your credit card ready and call

Toll free: (877) 421-READ (7323)

or send $18.00* each plus $5.95 S&H** to

WinePress Publishing
PO Box 428
Enumclaw, WA 98022

or order online at: www.winepressbooks.com

*Washington residents, add 8.4% sales tax

**add $1.50 S&H for each additional book ordered